EXPERT TO ENTREPRENEUR

JEFFREY P. KIPLINGER PHD

EXPERT

TO

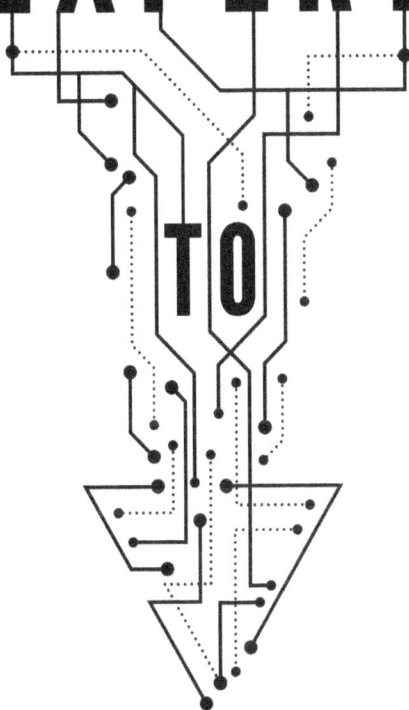

ENTREPRENEUR

HOW TO TURN YOUR HARD-WON
EXPERTISE INTO A THRIVING BUSINESS

HOUNDSTOOTH
PRESS

EXPERT TO ENTREPRENEUR
How to Turn Your Hard-Won Expertise into a Thriving Business

FIRST EDITION

ISBN   978-1-5445-4166-2 *Hardcover*
         978-1-5445-4167-9 *Paperback*
         978-1-5445-4168-6 *Ebook*

This book is dedicated to my wife, Katy. I am conscious, every single day, that I would never have made it here without her love, encouragement, and belief in me.

CONTENTS

PREFACE

This book is titled *Expert to Entrepreneur* for a good reason. There are professionals in many fields who, having put in their time and paid their dues in education and work experience, realize their expertise has great value to others. You probably bought this book because you are an expert in your field. You wonder how you might start a business and profit by delivering your product—your valuable idea based on your ability to do something very well—to others. But because you've been working and learning primarily in your field, you don't know how to start and succeed in business. This book is for you.

Many of my colleagues and clients offer their expertise in the form of services. Some develop patentable ideas from their rich experience and go on to found companies that make proprietary products. Either way, you will benefit from the business knowledge this book presents, as it is laid out in logical order from start to growth to the finish line. Founding a company requires great energy and commitment. Often alone at the outset, if successful you will be rewarded. Whether you intend to find investors or partners down the road, or do it on your own, you will take risks in this adventure.

This book is organized into three sections: "Starting," "Growing," and "Succeeding." The first, "Starting" is most pertinent if you are in the planning or investigative phases, or in the first year or so of startup. The second section. "Growing" is about turning your company into a stable, sustainable entity with a value of its own—beyond the value of you, the founder. The third, "Succeeding" is about fine-tuning that sustainable entity to optimize value, and how to turn that success into value for you and your family. The most common way to do the latter is by selling your company. If you're not there yet, no worries— this book may become a reference you can come back to again and again as you progress.

INTRODUCTION

All my life I wanted to run my own business. It's not that I wanted to start my career off as an entrepreneur—I saw the value of first following a career path like my peers. I got a PhD in organic chemistry, worked in a couple of postdoctoral research positions, and got my first "real job" at Pfizer, the pharmaceutical company, in 1989. I've always had a bit of a problem with authority, and as I developed skills and confidence in whatever I was doing, I arrogantly thought I could do a better job if I were to be my own boss. But working at Pfizer was fun, at least in the first few years, so it was easy to talk myself out of taking the big risk of giving up the salary and benefits to go out on my own.

At Pfizer, I invented and developed some cool technologies that changed the way the whole pharmaceutical industry approached the discovery and development of new drugs. I worked with a lot of scientists I admired—people way smarter than I was. Getting comfortable, I began to think I could make a nice thirty-year career and retire from there. But corporations, pharma firms included, tend to become behemoths capable of controlling their supply chains and increasing earnings by massive spending on marketing. In the pharmaceutical arena, internal research and development (R&D), where my colleagues and I worked, was no longer the engine that kept these companies healthy and growing. A lot of my friends left the company. Soon I came into conflict with management, which I felt devalued the contributions of top scientists—like me, of course. After a decade at Pfizer, I was fired.

Several years of false starts followed. *Should I get another job? Do I consult? Or should I really try to start a company?* After my firing, I lost confidence in myself. Everything I tried felt like a half commitment, a half risk. My ambivalence was without a doubt visible to potential employers and potential investors.

I tried a couple of semientrepreneurial ventures. One was a technology development center near the East Coast pharma hub in Boston, funded by a midwestern engineering firm that was developing a pharma equipment business. This was a nice way to run my own shop with someone else's funds! But despite the business growth that the parent company got from our efforts, the plug was pulled on our operation after the 9/11 attacks in 2001, when many customers froze spending and the United States entered a recession.

My wife at the time became frustrated with my attempts to get something off the ground. I tried consulting. Discouraged and ill-equipped to sell myself properly, I failed to build out a consulting sales pipeline. I earned at best half of what I should have—half of what my peers in the corporate world earned. I had given up on myself. My marriage failed, mostly due to my faltering self-esteem. I was in a self-pity spiral.

Eventually I had the proverbial "come to Jesus" talk with myself, and I realized I was luckier than a lot of people. I had, in the course of my career, surrounded myself with talented people, good friends, and smart colleagues. Luck favors the well-prepared, and experience and knowledge are simply ways by which we position ourselves to leverage luck. Keep that in mind as you read this book!

One day, a consulting client told me they had been out-sourcing a specific type of chromatography service to a contract services lab at the rate of $250,000 per year (for chiral molecule purification, and it does not matter at all if you know what that is). The contractor had just notified my client that the lab was closing and going out of business. My client, frustrated, asked if I knew of a lab that could take on this work.

It turned out the contractor had overextended with inves-tors, and the investors pulled the plug—suddenly. I was sure the contractor must have left a lot of other customers hanging and not just my client. Coincidentally, I had managed a lab at Pfizer that did this kind of work. I wondered if I could, and if I should, try to build a business that could capture those abandoned contracts.

I liked my client and their scientific team, and I asked for a couple of days to think about it. With no prior planning on my part, the work was mine if I could put something together. I had a ready-made customer waving a large pile of money at me if I could only set up what I had always wanted: a shop of my own. I made some phone calls and put together a plan. I had no idea what I was doing, but I knew I had a business.

What follows is everything I learned along my journey from dreamer to founder to CEO to seller—a successful cycle from startup to growth to exit strategy. Many books deal with one of these phases—each phase is deep enough to justify volumes. However, this is not a cursory guide. It deals specifically with the challenges I faced, and that you will face, as an expert tran-sitioning to an entrepreneur.

If you're like me—a deeply educated scientist or engineer with an entrepreneurial spirit, a taste for risk, and hunger to achieve something based on guts and intelligence—contained herein is all the nuts-and-bolts stuff that will help you turn your expertise into a business.

Your objective as an entrepreneur is to create something bigger than yourself. This book is not about selling your expertise directly as a consultant. It's about creating a company through which you and your employees deliver services or products at a scale beyond your capacity to do so as a one-person operation. You will learn to work *on* your company rather than *in* your company. By doing so, your company will develop into an entity that has value in and of itself—a value far beyond your value as the founding expert.

If you succeed, you will generate income and wealth, you will enjoy success in your own heart and in the eyes of your peers, and you will have built something that functions like a well-oiled machine. At some point you will retire or walk away, and the company will go on.

Read and follow this book's first two sections, "Starting" and "Growing," to reach that goal: the independently valuable company. If at that point you choose to take your return on all the time and effort you've invested, you will be ready to exit. The final section is called "Succeeding," because being paid for what you created is a quantitative measure of your success. In my last company, completing the cycle from startup to growth to exit took more than ten years. It can be a long journey, but the three sections herein break it down in a way that makes the journey understandable.

I introduce quite a few concepts covered in other business books, but I orient them to meet the perspective of a scientist or engineer with deep specialist knowledge and little classical business training. I spend more time than most such books do on marketing and selling, as these areas are often neglected by highly analytical and objective professionals, who believe their capabilities and expertise should speak for themselves.

To help you achieve optimal success, I offer a concept I call the *Four Value Signals*. These are guideposts for determining that your company has developed to the stage at which it operates without the direct involvement of you, the expert owner and founder. For this to be effective, the business functions must be met by your team, you must implement a specific sales process that consistently and efficiently brings the right customers, you must meet some basic benchmarks of financial health and strength, and…you must get out of the way. The Four Value Signals—Team, Sales Process, Financial Strength, and the Owner—are based on the aforementioned factors. These provide a way to determine whether you've done what you set out to do: to answer the age-old question, "Are we there yet?"

I am not writing for those who are perfectly happy working on somebody else's payroll for whatever reason—job security, family situations, a great employer. There is nothing wrong with deliberately and in good spirit choosing that path. It just isn't for me, and if you're reading this, maybe it isn't for you either.

This book does not sugarcoat the truth about the difficulties and risks in founding a company. Neither does it claim that I—or any of the other business owners I interviewed—have a special skill or talent that guaranteed success. Mostly what I had was an ability to calculate risk and tolerate it, as well as a dogged, often stubborn, unwillingness to fail.

I was lucky to have a customer at the ready, and lucky to know smart people who could help me. And although my wife and I later separated, thanks to her solid career I had health insurance, a good credit rating, and backup income during my startup year. As much as the separation hurt both of us, I was lucky to then meet my present wife, who believed in me through some tough years and always gives me strength. I was lucky to close some great deals and let go of others, and the experience helped me build a fantastic sales and marketing program. My company's success gained the attention of a buyer who had some exciting plans to expand, and the final sale of my company brought me good money for my ten-year investment.

This book is for professionals who have done their time intimately learning their field through advanced education and experience and want to trade on that expertise to create a valuable company. This brings to mind science, engineering, and technology professionals who travel a long path to be considered experts. Getting to the top of these highly specialized fields requires intense work, which doesn't allow a lot of time for business education. If you are an expert with an inner entrepreneur, I hope that by reading this you will learn to position yourself to leverage your hard-earned expertise, benefit from luck, and stay open to possibilities in the face of challenges.

This is not an easy path, but the potential rewards are great. If you're willing to embark on this journey, you cannot fully cushion yourself from risk. Just resolve to meet it well-armed.

HOW TO USE THIS BOOK

I write about all aspects of starting, growing, and eventually exiting from a company built on expertise. However, not all readers will be at the same starting point. If you're prestartup, I suggest you spend time reading the first section, "Starting" as a manual or list of items to consider or ponder. Read the second section "Growing" to understand what direction you're going with your business.

If you've already started your business and are in the trenches, the first section on starting will help you cover bases you may have missed. But the section on growing will be most valuable, helping you set the goals you need to succeed.

If you've been operating for two or more years and feel like you have some stuff down on the business side (as opposed to the technical side), predominantly focus on the Growing and Succeeding sections. You need to have a destination in mind, and this will help you think about what you want, what you need to do to get that, and what the later stages look like. If, like many others, you hope to eventually sell to a strategic buyer—one who will place a high value on the company because of its expertise—read the section on succeeding well before you intend to sell.

As the book progresses, an increasing amount of time is dedicated to explaining how to apply the Four Value Signals. The concept is designed to help you build the dream of many business founders—a company that has value as an entity in and of itself, without you. Make no mistake, you don't have to choose to leave your company, but to those bitten by the business bug, this is the top of the success chain—your company is sustainable and scalable, and someone will pay good money for it. You don't have to accept the offer. A mature company is much more satisfying to run, so stay in business if you like and make it even more valuable.

No matter where you are in your entrepreneurial journey, you can pick up this book and get something from it...and continue to return to it as your company grows.

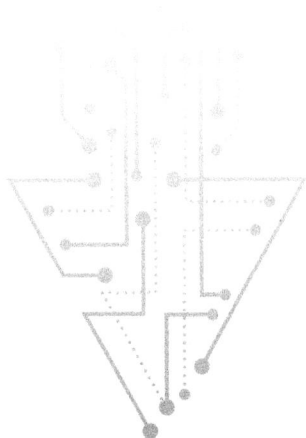

STARTING

"I guess what I'm trying to say is I don't think you can measure life in terms of years. I think longevity doesn't necessarily have anything to do with happiness. I mean happiness comes from facing challenges and going out on a limb and taking risks. If you're not willing to take a risk for something you really care about, you might as well be dead."

—DIANE FROLOV

"I have not failed. I've just found ten thousand ways it won't work."

—THOMAS A. EDISON

CHAPTER 1

WHY WE DO IT

What exactly are entrepreneurs?

We are a select group—and an important one! Early economist Adam Smith wrote in his book *The Wealth of Nations*, which was originally published in 1776, that entrepreneurship is key to global improvements in living standards.

Economists today narrowly define entrepreneurs, to make sure they study a similar sample set. Commonly, they separate the self-employed based on whether their businesses are incorporated or unincorporated, following the model of researchers David S. Evans and Linda S. Leighton.[1] The basic advantage of incorporation is that the company can assume liability as a unique legal entity separate from its owners. This has the effect of separating those for whom the business is a way of earning money from those for whom the business is intended to be, or to become, a financial asset. In this simplified model, an entrepreneur is someone who builds a business, as opposed to someone who works for hire.

Incorporation separates an owner from the business in

---

1   David S. Evans and Linda S. Leighton, "Some Empirical Aspects of Entrepreneurship," *American Economic Review* 79, no. 3 (June 1989): 519–535, https://www.jstor.org/stable/1806861.

important ways, facilitating growth and investment by means that an unincorporated entity cannot. While a corporation may pay its founder a salary, it also grows and retains earnings through processes that allow the owner to potentially accumulate wealth—similar to improving a home in a rising real estate market.

This book assumes you want to build a company that is intended to grow and become valuable as an entity. You don't need to immediately incorporate your business to put yourself in this group. There are legal structures that sort of straddle incorporated and unincorporated, and many companies progress from one structure to another as they grow. Such legal structures are discussed in the next couple of chapters. Here, let's talk about the entrepreneur—a much-studied beast who may fall somewhere between borderline sociopath and savior of our future economy.

THE ENTREPRENEUR PERSONALITY

Is there an entrepreneurial nature—a common set of traits that characterize entrepreneurs?

Maybe you're familiar with the Myers-Briggs Type Indicator personality assessment test. One of the sixteen possible personality types it identifies—ESTP (extraversion, sensing, thinking, prospecting)—is called the Entrepreneur. I personally test ENTJ (extraversion, intuition, thinking, judging), which labels me the Commander. Another business founder I know tests INFJ (introversion, intuition, feeling, judging), so his personality type is deemed the Counselor. And still another founder I know tests ISFP personality type—the Composer.

All three of us ran companies that provided analytical chemistry services. There seems to be plenty of room in the entrepreneur class, and within any field of science, for various personality types. Yet popular psychology seems to love defining the personality of the entrepreneur—virtually every business book, magazine, and online media outlet addresses the personality traits of this individual. That doesn't necessarily mean they converge on a conclusion.

We are passionate, resilient, flexible visionaries with a strong sense of self (according to features in *Forbes* magazine), as well as motivated, optimistic, creative risk-takers (so say authors of articles on Entrepreneur.com). We are determined yet open-minded self-starters, who are confident and competitive, with strong people skills and work ethic (according to Under30CEO.com content). Another Entrepreneur.com article paints entrepreneurs as being "all about the customer" and "able to sell themselves." They "make big decisions carefully," despite being "not afraid of risk."

If I were to write such an article, I would perhaps throw in adjectives like "aggressive" or "stubborn." I might point to cultural and family history as influential factors. I'd likely also note that a good number of entrepreneurs act—rationally—with their partner or family to achieve a long-term strategy of diversification or economic hedging: one family member might have a protected position, a hefty savings portfolio, or simply a solid job with health insurance, so the budding entrepreneur can take on more risk, thus providing the family with potential for a more diverse plan for wealth accumulation.

In my view, the makeup of an entrepreneur is a multivariate equation.

Real research generally concurs.[2] Personality is regarded

2   Sari Pekkala Keer, William R. Kerr, and Tina Xu, "Personality Traits of Entrepreneurs: A Review of Recent Literature" (*NBER Working Paper Series* no. 24097, December 2017), https://doi.org/10.3386/w24097.

as a series of scales and may be categorized to some extent by differences between groups on those scales (e.g., tolerance of uncertainty). However, even researchers disagree on which traits might be attributive to personality and which are considered skills or skillsets. Think, for example, of risk tolerance: is it an innate trait, or can it be learned?

It's probably best not to speculate on what traits drive an individual to take on the responsibility and risk of starting a business, and to avoid the debate about whether entrepreneurs are born or made. However, some interesting commonalities have been observed among successful founders—again, those who chose to incorporate their businesses. Demographically, they tend to be educated white males from financially stable two-parent families. This says far more about our culture and groups that enjoy greater privilege than it does about what makes them entrepreneurially spirited or driven.

An interesting observation in a recent study is that entrepreneurs are much more likely to score high on learning aptitude tests *and* much more likely to have engaged in illicit activity during adolescence. The authors conclude in part that the "smart and illicit" trait combination is a strong sorting factor for those who found and incorporate businesses. The researchers conclude, "To create and introduce novel products under risky and uncertain conditions and 'destroy' the positions of incumbent firms, it is unsurprising that the...entrepreneur is self-confident, smart, and prone to challenging convention."[3]

What can be said about us scientists, engineers, or deep technical experts? We certainly often group with people labeled "smart" and "driven." Correlation is not causation, but we definitely correlate with "motivated," "a self-starter," and

---

3   Ross Levine and Yona Rubinstein, "Smart and Illicit: Who Becomes an Entrepreneur and Do They Earn More?" (*NBER Working Paper Series* no. 19276, August 2013), https://doi.org/10.3386/w19276.

"competitive"—traits typically needed to achieve our professional positions.

When we look around at the business founders we envy—wishing we could take their leap, wondering if we should and if we have what it takes—we see a mix of creativity, risk tolerance, competitiveness, and faith in oneself. These traits alone do not make us entrepreneurs—they don't include hard work, commitment, and a hundred skills we need to learn—but they give us core strengths that provide a fairly firm launchpad.

BORN OR MADE?

It's clear that your background—the environment in which you were raised, were educated, and became mature—is a determinant in success as an entrepreneur. This is the "nurture" component of the nature-versus-nurture discussion. As with so many other goals, you have a greater chance of achievement if you have a positive example from your background.

If your family has some wealth or your parents were highly paid, you are statistically much more likely to earn a good living. If your parents are artists by profession, you have a greater chance of being successful in creative fields. Social scientists believe that a good example of success observed during your upbringing tends to limit or remove some psychological barriers, such as self-doubt. Observable, up-close success also serves as a template, so you know the steps you could take to achieve. It becomes easier to choose your path and—most important—to start.

Starting a business involves some personal risk. The financial risk is high enough that many aspiring entrepreneurs decide their responsibilities as parents, partners, and providers mean the risk of destabilizing their home situation outweighs the possible rewards. There is personal risk in failure, too—risk that others might see you as unsuccessful and form negative opinions of your capability. We value the opinions of friends, family, and colleagues, and we may even feel that a failed entrepreneurial venture might negatively impact our ability to reenter the workforce. Failure can injure the psyche and sense of self.

Let me also address a social reality. It is true that, historically, wealth, education, and being a white male correlate positively with successful entrepreneurship. If we as a society accept that these factors expose the fact that *not* being white, male, educated, and well-connected are real barriers to business success, we've exposed a structural problem that needs to be addressed for the successful future of our world. Every population is becoming more diverse as people connect more widely, and a privileged class with greater opportunity is not sustainable. We cannot accept that someone's personal environment—the nurture factor—contributes strongly to their business success without recognizing that our overarching business environment needs to favor everyone equally.

A final nature-versus-nurture point worth examining is the dominance of corporate culture in shaping our view of the business world and ourselves. Particularly in the years since World War II, big corporations have been seen as the apotheosis of capitalist success. Corporate giants like Sony, General Electric, Merck, ADM, Nestlé, and others represent success on a grand and global scale that had few equals among earlier generations.

We resent and revere the achievement of companies like these, often hating their market dominance, control of the flow of goods, and manipulation of our preference or need for their products. Their supply chains link to the most remote parts of the world, exploiting the inequality between developed and underdeveloped societies. These corporations have done so partly by crafting a dominating mythology: that everyone is paid fairly, that hierarchical management systems are the most efficient, that ownership in the hands of a few enhances everyone's lives, that taxes are way too high, and that we shouldn't question intent in the face of success.

Whether you have a philosophical view of this, seeing it as right or wrong, admit this to yourself as a budding entrepreneur: the big corporate world has a lot of control over how we view ourselves. This is worth examining. Do you feel the management hierarchy in big companies, maybe the one where you work, is really based on merit? Do you think everyone is paid equitably for the same contributions, or would management feel threatened if all employees knew one another's salaries? Do you have the impression that executives in big companies are exceptionally smart and make very complex decisions by superior reasoning—or do they just wing it to the best of their ability, like you do?

If you pull back the curtain on the myths global corporations use to keep their workforces in line, you may be able to better gauge your own ability to start and run a successful business.

From the beginning I felt I could really demonstrate, really show my clients true ROI (return on investment). The agency I was working for never wanted to do that, because they were quite literally scared they wouldn't be able to—they just didn't know how. And I was doing most of their business development! The clients were all asking how we were going to know if this was the right investment, and my company didn't have an answer. I started to think about a different model of matchmaking and measurement together. Eventually I realized if there was going to be a better way, I had to be the one to do it.

Laura Browne

CEO, Covalent Bonds

GETTING THE LOVE YOU WANT

Have you ever felt that only you can see the value of what you bring to your employer?

When the company hired you, management recognized your strengths—your field of study in university, the papers you published, the reputation you developed as a contributor or thought leader among your peers. The hard work you've put in during your years with the organization has had an observable impact. Your colleagues appreciate your ideas, and you can see your contribution in the advancing projects around you. Yet the faceless business treats you as if you're part of a bigger machine, paying you a salary commensurate with industry norms, not with your contribution. Every now and then, someone from above sends down an "attaboy." Your boss has dealt with lots of underlings who feel the way you do and is tired of listening to them ask for recognition beyond what they are so generously given.

Maybe, you think, *I should take this show on the road. What I do is not completely unique, but I'm really good at it, and there are dozens, probably even hundreds, of others who would pay for it. Just last week, I was talking with Jean. She worked here ten years ago. She went out on her own and set up a lab, and now we send work to her for three times what it used to cost us to do it in-house. Why shouldn't I do the same thing? I can see the company is going toward more and more outsourcing, and I know what I do is worth money.*

You know your skills, talents, or innovative ideas are worth money. You know people who would pay you. You know some associates who are already successful as entrepreneurs. You wonder if you, too, could successfully break out on your own.

You're not the only expert who sees the opportunity to be an entrepreneur. What *might* make you different is your ability to objectively evaluate your expertise and skills as potential generators of revenue. If you're selling your skills rather than an invention, your company will deliver services to customers or clients.

Business opportunities track the larger industry cycles, coming and going according to market trends. What is your potential customer doing now? Are they outsourcing in this area or that? Has this technology become a routine commodity of little value, or does it have the potential to bring new opportunities for a customer? What is the established competition doing—jumping into your market or ignoring the opportunity you noticed?

Is there a large value created for each customer (high profit margin), or will you need to have many customers before you see a profit (low margin)? If you're in a low-margin business, how will you access the many customers you need in order to break even before you run out of cash? If it's a high-margin offering with a high price, how will you convince select customers to take a big money risk on your new company? How much money might it take to get your business started? How long, realistically, would it take to recoup that money?

This is the time to leverage the skills you developed in learning to be an expert in your field: research, analysis, and testing. There are many things to think about before you start, and we will talk about developing a business plan.

For now, ask yourself this important question: *I know I have value, but can I sell it to the necessary number of customers in this market, using my skills and drive?*

Early in my career in big pharma, I was able to satisfy internal customers and be productive—better than most. But I kept encountering resistance and getting in trouble. One boss told me to slow down, because I moved so fast he couldn't keep up with my progress. He felt threatened that I was getting noticed by others.

A friend and mentor who had started his own company said, "You're not built for a large company. I'm surprised you survived this long." He was encouraging me to go out on my own. So many opportunities were eternally on hold due to my fear of taking risks.

I was raised to think that taking a risk was a good thing, that it makes you stronger and you learn from failure. Growing and running a business is mostly about risk assessment and risk-taking.

Still, I didn't make the jump until my company suddenly shut down our research site. At age forty-four, with four young children, I decided it was now or never. I declined a large pay raise to join a consulting group and jumped into a world I was unfamiliar with: self-employment and starting a business.

Dr. Joseph Simpkins

Founder, Virscidian Inc.

READY FOR A PUSH

I've heard people refer to major, unexpected changes in life—such as being fired—as signs or omens, messages that they should pursue a new opportunity. I seem to meet a lot of talented, creative people who have been fired from jobs. In my experience, talented, ambitious, out-of-the-box thinkers get fired frequently, especially from big corporations!

I know top scientists who, after getting the boot, opened bakeries and photography businesses, and earned MFA degrees with the intent to write or paint. One scientist I know started a sawmill. In almost every case, however, they were back in a scientific role within five years, usually at a more senior level. The emotional upheaval of a perceived failure is *not necessarily* a sign that you should change careers.

Something about a big change often makes people feel free, yet freedom without structure is simply unanchored. It's probably not wise to start a business in the wake of a divorce, a traumatic job loss, or the death of an immediate family member. Yes, these things free us from responsibility and cause us to question our path, but the self-realignment that needs to happen in the wake of such huge losses leaves little mental energy to move forward for a while.

Instead of waiting for a liberating event (or personal tragedy) to push you off a cliff before you decide to realize your dream, what if you were more active in planning ahead? Instead consider the possibility of less traumatic nudges that might help you consciously make the jump. In my case, I was nudged when one of my consulting clients lost access to a provider of key services. My client was spending $250,000 per year for that provider, who suddenly closed shop in the wake of a bad financial decision. With a ready customer and knowledge that there were more, I jumped. I asked my client, "What if I were to do that work for you?"

What unexpected event could you be ready for? A ready customer with a well-defined need? A great-aunt with an unexpectedly large bequest from her estate? A spouse or partner who lands a dream job in another state, so the two of you are relocating for a fresh start backed up by a healthy family income? How about a lottery win? Don't laugh—this happened to a business partner of mine!

As the saying goes, chance favors the prepared mind. Picture me saying this to you as a friend: "Please don't start your business because you were fired, or in the wake of a divorce. I feel awful for you, and I've been there. Take some time to recover from the trauma, and approach this kind of life decision with clearer eyes."

During the years before I jumped into starting my first business, it was very difficult for me to ascertain whether my desire to be my own boss was real and strong enough to get me there. I needed to figure out if my desire was directed toward succeeding, or if I was just whining about being unhappy in my present employment. It took me years to start down the road to entrepreneurship. Fears and rationalizations held me back. Even after the strong push of being fired, even with no kids and a gainfully employed spouse as a backstop, I was afraid of failure.

What supported me internally, helping me push past the fears and inevitable failures, was a strong desire to win. Somehow, especially when I felt stuck or others didn't believe in me, I tried harder. "I'll show them" may be an unhealthy self-motivation tool, but it worked for me.

Never lose sight of how personal and emotional the decision can be to become an entrepreneur. Making pros-versus-cons lists, business plans, and spreadsheets might help you vet your ideas and start stronger, but you still have to walk to the edge and jump. Perhaps you've already taken that leap, or maybe you're still pondering. Ready or not, read on!

KEY TAKEAWAYS FROM CHAPTER 1

- There may or may not be such a thing as a natural-born entrepreneur, but there are personal strengths you probably have in common with some successful entrepreneurs.
- As an expert, you likely possess strong abilities to analyze opportunities and calculate risks. These are valuable skills in an entrepreneur's toolbox!
- Chance favors the prepared mind: if you've done some homework and thought experiments, you'll know when the universe is pushing you to take a leap.

CHAPTER 2

WHAT TO THINK ABOUT BEFORE YOU JUMP

Maybe you're reading this as the owner of a startup. Perhaps you're between jobs and contemplating starting something instead of reentering the workforce. Or maybe you're stuck in a corporate job so unsatisfying that you're thinking about getting out and chasing the entrepreneurial dream.

If the first two sound like you, this chapter will help you progress more quickly and with greater confidence through your early growth phases.

If the last one describes you, jumping out of a stable paying gig into the unknown is risky and scary. You want to pack your parachute carefully and test your equipment. You can't plan for everything, but checking that chute surely makes your jump safer. This chapter gives you some things to think about and do before handing your boss your resignation letter, and it will help you hit the ground running when you finally jump.

THE HEART OF YOU

When did drafting mission, vision, values, and purpose statements become a thing? It's standard, in a business context, for every good corporation to craft such statements. Corporate management guru Peter Drucker was probably the first to apply the term "mission statement" in a business context, in his book *Management: Tasks, Responsibilities, Practices*, which was first published in 1973. By the mid-1980s the business world was saturated with articles about mission statements. By 1990, the vision statement was also customary, along with the values statement. The purpose statement came along a little later, and the inexorable march from useful to eye-rolling began.

I stipulate that a herd mentality and a certain amount of nonsense are present in this practice. I read one mission statement that boldly declared, "Our mission is to serve our customers with the best services at a fair price and to profit from them so that we can reward our employees." *Really?* Selling services at a profit and paying employees—that's the definition of a business, not a mission.

Values statements are often just as offbeat.

Big companies (in my former industry, I think of Pfizer, Merck, or Biogen) are powerful because they optimize all of their business functions around a single principle—let's call it "maximum efficiency." Products compete in the marketplace according to efficiency factors, such as the cost to manufacture and distribute, the customer's perception of quality or efficacy, and the ability of the company's messaging to reach its targets. Companies do *not* compete by leveraging their values or doing business with people with whom they are philosophically and ethically aligned. In fact, despite surveys that show a declining view of the ethical principles of large companies in virtually all industries over the last few decades, customers still buy their products. These companies continue to expand and become more successful.

Yet all of these behemoths have lists of five to seven values, which anyone can find on the corporate websites. Usually, these include words like "integrity," "service," and "respect." It's not made clear as to how these companies put these values into practice, and it's usually possible to find obvious and public examples of when they haven't. My point is that *values don't matter if you do not intend to leverage your values for company growth*. A set of corporate values has, for many company executives, become a box to tick—for reasons identical to those that require a US political candidate to wear a flag pin on their lapel. For big corporations, values are reduced to a tick box the marketing team must check. Touting company values is thought to bring some basic level of credibility.

I insist, though, that writing down and checking in with your personal values is an important step for a founder. First, recognize that *you* are the company you founded, at least until it grows to become an independent entity. You will have a much better chance of accomplishing your goals if you set out to take actions that align with your personal values. Second, you'll find and keep better employees—and customers—if your values are shared. Values don't determine leadership style. Instead, self-awareness and the ability to communicate personal values to others inspire those who share similar values.

President Harry Truman said, "You can never tell what's going to happen to a man until he gets to a place of responsibility. You just can't tell in advance, whether you're talking about a general in the field or a manager of a large farm or a bank officer or a president…You've just got to pick the man you think is best on the basis of his past history and the views he expresses."

Imagine that, rather than founding, you are being nominated to lead your company. How do you express the parts of your character that will convince those you work with, and for, that you will be a good leader?

Here's a way to start to understand which values are most important to you. Type "list of values" into a search engine. The links will lead to lists of words like "truth" or "teamwork." These are your prompts. From these words, pick twelve to fifteen that most resonate with you. Read your picks, look for overlaps, and reduce your list until you end up with three to five you feel are the most important.

Try to capture what appeals to you about each word by restating it in a sentence, such as "We are *generous* with our time and energy when we work with others." Write your values down, and revisit them periodically. I know a CEO who meets weekly with his leadership team and always asks these two questions: "What did we do that best illustrated a value?" and "Where did we fail to operate according to our values?" The values you share become the operating principles of your company and the foundation of its culture.

Vision statements, like mission statements and values statements, can be trite and meaningless in big corporations. For a smaller company, though, vision is a principle of direction for a team. Think in concrete terms: *Where do I want to be in, say, two or three years? What does my company look like physically? How many people? What does my facility look like? What do customers see and feel when they visit? What's my revenue? What have I built and added to make the company more efficient and profitable?*

In other words, *visualize your vision* in detail, and write it down. This is the company you are going to build. No vision, no goals, no roadmap, no destination—without a vision you aren't necessarily lost, but you're directionless.

That brings us to purpose. Your purpose statement is essentially your *why*—your reason for starting the company, the unique worth you bring to the world. Why you've chosen to build your business is related closely to the way your customer will perceive you. Inspirational speaker Simon Sinek talks about the importance of this in his 2009 book, *Start with Why: How Great Leaders Inspire Everyone to Take Action*, and his "Start with Why" TED Talk.

Sinek makes the case that most companies talk about *what* they do, and to differentiate they may talk about *how* they do it and how they're different. Few companies communicate their essential, inspiring *why*—their reason for being in business. If you establish your company's purpose, you will discover customers who also feel its importance and inspiration. They will buy from you, believe in you, continue to do business with you, and refer to you. One of Sinek's examples is Apple. *What* does Apple do? It makes consumer electronics. But the company's *why* is so much more. Apple leads with the belief that its team can design beautiful objects that bring exciting and inspiring technology to users.

In my last company, we offered analytical chemistry services to companies developing new drugs (*what*). We had some unique technologies that gave us an edge in speed and quality (*how*). We believed our way of doing this work helped our customers make better decisions early in drug development, saving time and money, and increasing the value of their products to people who needed it (*why*).

The *why* was the cornerstone of our approach in speaking to customers: "If we can get you more of your drug, will you be able to do more testing on it?" "If we get you higher purity, will your assay results be more reliable?" "If this method works, we can help you scale it up to produce material for your clinical trial."

Mission Statement	What does your company do, defined in terms of the value it provides your customers?	Two to three sentences max, no jargon	All personnel know and believe that this is what you do, your mission.
Values Statement	What do you most believe in that drives you to be in business?	Three to five value words with a sentence for each	This is posted on the wall in full view, and values are reality-checked regularly.
Vision Statement	What does your company look like in two to three years, in detail?	Bullet list or a descriptive paragraph	Revisit your vision quarterly to write near-term objectives.
Purpose Statement	What is your core reason for being in business—your company's essential "why"?	One to two sentences tops so it's brief but to the point	All personnel know the company's purpose, using it to craft messaging to connect with customers.

Most experts go into business with the belief that they offer their experience and skills to the customer. While that is true, it's not enough. Your customers do not buy your expertise or work with you because of your résumé or your lab's equipment. They buy whatever product or service provides a benefit to them—a savings, the removal of a problem, a reduction in worry, an outsourcing of something that bores them. This is important: *your customers do not care about what you do—they care about what's in it for them.*

You will truly connect with a customer only if you understand each other. They need to know you *get* them. You'll learn to say, "I understand what you're trying to achieve," instead of, "We do this service and that." The closer you align with their way of seeing the world, the more likely you are to achieve that connection.

I've just given you a simple way of looking at your personal ideology as a path toward creating the best business you can.

Don't overthink it, but do hold on to it. You do not have to fully define your mission, values, vision, or purpose statements to get started, but internalize ideas that are important to you. Put your heart into your business as much as you do your mind.

In business, you will succeed or fail based on your ability to clearly define your business and your customer. This is not the same as defining your product or service, especially if others provide the same products and services. What you have that is unique comes from your beliefs, your convictions, and your reasons for being in business. Understanding these, building on them, and hiring employees and recruiting customers based on these factors bring you much greater success than that of competitors who are industrially focused but not heart-centered.

Values make a huge difference to the way you operate. We were three partners when we started. In terms of experience and knowledge, we complemented each other very well—we covered all the bases. But problems arose due to differing values.

There were conflicts from the very beginning. While we always agreed that it was very good to have partners, the partnership needed to be actively managed. There were constant ups and downs. This was something we should have paid more attention to at the outset.

Dr. Michael Kouchakdjian

Founder, Blue Stream Laboratories

YOUR NICHE

In planning to develop a business around your technical expertise, you realize others in your field have done the same. They are your direct competitors. By starting before you, they already have customers, some of whom are quite happy. Some competitors may be so successful that they've grown, and by word of mouth or successful marketing, have an established brand with a favorable reputation. Whether or not your intended customers have worked with them, they likely know who your biggest direct competitors are. You, however, will be an unknown entity up against competition that has a well-known reputation and name recognition.

While you may not have a completely unique product or service, you have *something* different to offer. Maybe you feel you can bring a customer higher quality or faster delivery. Maybe you feel competitors misunderstand their impact just enough that you can tweak the process to better fit a need. Maybe you feel you are easier to work with, because you and the customer have shared values. Maybe your reputation as the go-to expert in your application area tops all pretenders to the throne. If you didn't believe you have the ability to deliver to a customer something they are not already getting, you would not have conceived this business.

Whatever qualities you feel give you an edge over your competition are critical to your success. But being more expert than your competitor is not important in itself. What's important is the subset of customers who believe it—combined with their desire to work with the expert. This group of customers, who want the quality, need the speed, or feel much better working with a top expert, is your ideal target. What you do for them, specifically for them, is your *niche*.

You should be able to recognize and articulate your niche, that market in which you are unique. You should be able to describe your niche in very few words. You should understand where to find customers in your target market. Knowing your niche and how to access your prospective clients within it helps guide you as you start up your business. As Orville Redenbacher, the food scientist turned popcorn magnate, famously said, "Do one thing, and do it better than anyone else." Knowing your niche helps you know if you're on plan.

Now let's talk about market, finding your ideal customer, and your value to them, as we go deeper into building your business.

GO TO MARKET

To describe your early plans to market and sell your goods, I'll use a term that's common in the investing world. If you're talking to professional investors at any level, they'll likely ask about your "go-to-market strategy." This is relatively recent vocabulary, lumping together pricing strategy, customer profile, value proposition, messaging, marketing plan, and a half dozen more of last year's terms.

Before you jump, you need to do some thinking about these things, but you will probably not have all the answers and some of your work will be educated guessing. A go-to-market plan is the tactics you intend to use to launch, sell, and increase sales of your service. Its foundation is the research you've done about your customer and your competition. This includes understanding the benefit customers get by buying from you, and knowing what they will probably pay. From there, and over time, you'll build a specific plan to find your ideal customer, demonstrate to them why what you offer is valuable, and sell your goods to them at a profit.

Of course, you can't know everything, at least not in a complete and clear fashion, before you actually start your business. Your go-to-market strategy requires some thought and adjusting. Investors ask about your go-to-market strategy not because they expect you to know everything, but because they want to know you've thought about all of the marketing elements and are doing the necessary work to validate your ideas.

Research firm CB Insights recently examined startup failures postmortem and found that 42 percent failed due to lack of a market need.[4] As it turns out, a large proportion of companies fail to sufficiently study their market and prospective customer base prior to launch.

A fully developed go-to-market strategy includes some examination of the following six topics. Do not aim for "fully developed" at this stage, but try to think through what you know and don't know about each of these points:

1. **Your business strategy.** Why is launching these services important?
2. **Your market.** Who are the ideal customers, how will you reach them, what do you need them to know, what value will you create for them, and what will compel them to buy?
3. **Pricing.** What are the costs to produce, current market pricing, and your pricing strategy—for example, low-cost or premium?
4. **Marketing plan.** What direction will you take in corporate and personal branding, as well as processes, channels, and budget for marketing your goods?
5. **Sales and support process.** How do you plan to bring the customer to the point of purchase, and how will you support them so they become repeat buyers?
6. **Success metrics.** Yes, total sales is one, but have you thought about your measures for customer acquisition and repeating with your company, too?

If you haven't already been thinking to some extent about all of the above, I'm surprised. Most founding experts have a pretty

4   CB Insights, *The Top 20 Reason Startups Fail*, 2021, https://s3-us-west-2.amazonaws.com/cbi-content/research-reports/The-20-Reasons-Startups-Fail.pdf.

good idea of how their offering provides value to a customer. The gaps in their strategy, if any, are often in clearly defining that customer, developing a marketing plan, and defining success. The reason to think through any of these six things is *focus*. The more you are focused—surgically focused—the more likely you are to accomplish your projected achievement. Whether your go-to-market plan is fully developed or not, keep refining your strategy as you gain experience with your business!

World War II General George Patton famously said about strategic plans, "A good plan, violently executed now, is better than a perfect plan next week." This reminds me not to over-think things, and perhaps it will do the same for you. I wrote this book for an audience of experts who tend to be highly educated and deeply, rather than broadly, skilled. Within our fields we are the best, and we often get to that level of expertise by using our unusually active minds. If anyone can overthink a problem, it is us experts.

PLANNING TO MAKE SALES

Often when we imagine what our budding company will look like—the activity, the office or lab, the staff—we picture the operations end of the business, the activities that deliver our products or services to our customers. In our mind's eye, we see the technicians and their instruments or computers, the scientists manipulating 3D data sets on multiple monitors, or the engineers with CAD design plans and renderings. We seem to rarely picture the activity of sales, of acquiring the customer—and, of course, this must happen before we can deliver anything and collect payment.

Highly analytical and objective individuals—like you—tend to *hate* selling. People like us will do almost anything to avoid selling, and that includes forgetting that sales are important. We tend to distrust and feel manipulated by marketing concepts, because we are trained to be skeptical and pick things apart for hidden meanings. Anything that smells sales-y pushes us toward our professional skills in analysis. And when we buy, we feel we do so based on carefully researched objective criteria. If we hate being sold to, we loathe having to sell to someone else. The very thought makes us cringe.

For a business without a customer, there's nothing to deliver, no revenue, and therefore no money to pay employees and buy machines. Your future employees may spend 100 percent of their time producing, but you will have to spend much of your time, likely *most* of your time, on acquiring customers and keeping them happy. Acquiring clientele is challenging work, so if you have customers who will buy from you and then buy again, you'll save yourself some effort. But make no mistake, you will always need to attract a steady stream of customers.

I'll dedicate a lot of airtime, so to speak, on how to sell with honesty, credibility, and respect for yourself and your customers. I understand that delivering to customers is easy for you, but acquiring customers is more challenging.

You will start your business with a good vision of how your operation will deliver. But in the beginning, you will probably know little about who your potential customers are, how much they need you, what they need from you, how much they will pay, and how to keep them coming back. A little work, to develop a clear customer profile and a sales process before you start, will pay dividends later. Just as you know you need an equipment budget, supplies, and some space to operate from, you need to plan to market and sell your service or product. There are several things you can do that will help prestartup.

Who is your *ideal* customer? Simply defined, an ideal customer is one who gets the most value from working with you—they need your expertise, you make a big impact, they pay a premium for your help, they buy from you again, and they recommend you to others. You may think that just offering your products or services, if you market them effectively, will bring ideal customers to you. After all, isn't that what your website is supposed to do?

Most entrepreneurs' websites showcase information about their technical approach and expertise. This is great because it saves you from having to explain in detail what you do. But website content doesn't address that goal of connecting with the ideal customer. First, the more broadly you pitch at the market, the fewer customers you'll find. Targeting a narrow segment you know best connects you with the people you're best set up to help, and this is hard to do with a website. Second, a customer who isn't a perfect fit for your company may buy once, but the perfect fit will come back again and again, saving you endless effort in sales and marketing. Finding reasons you're the perfect fit is your job, not your website's.

What will that ideal customer gain from you, and can you quantify that gain? To test this, define your ideal customer according to your best guess, locate a few matches (or get an introduction or referral), and call them. Yes, actually call the prospective customer on the phone. Tell them your plans to enter the market, ask if they think that would be useful to them or others they know, and find out if they feel your pricing is appropriate. Ask directly, "How much do you think this is worth?"

That last step may make you feel uncomfortable. You're asking a potential customer to help you understand why they might buy. Sounds suspiciously like selling, right? You're thinking, *Hey, wait, I thought I didn't have to worry about the horrible selling part until I got up and running! This isn't fair!*

Stop, and take a breath. You are asking not for money but for insight. You're trying to understand to what degree you might be useful in the marketplace. Imagine you're a cab driver and you stop to pick up a fare. Wouldn't you like to know where they're going, and maybe some other value-based criteria such as whether they're in a big hurry?

When I started my first independent lab, I got this same advice: get out and talk to potential customers. I made it easy by never asking if they were interested in buying from me. Instead, I framed every conversation around vetting my business idea: "Would you help me out by letting me ask a bunch of questions about your experience with this kind of thing? I want to try to make as few mistakes as possible, and I value your experienced point of view." Every single person I talked to, somewhere in the conversation, either expressed an interest in working with me ("Call me as soon as you're set up; I know we could use some help") or offered to refer me to someone they knew.

Try to prime these potential customers for a future sales conversation. Just ask if they'd like to hear from you again when you're close to being operational. You might have some rough idea of *when* you might be able to serve them, at least in which calendar quarter you'll start operations. Your contacts know it will take a little while to start up.

They will likely not be willing to sign a contract a year from your start date, but they may sign a services agreement once they have assurance that you're actually going to start. Services agreements are common when larger companies start relationships with service providers, to stipulate contract terms, deliverables, and confidentiality. Having a services agreement in place makes it easier for the customer to contract with you as soon as you're operational and they have a need. It serves as a bridge to future sales discussions.

This research might result in several ready-to-go customers anxious to work with you from day one. If so, try at this stage to quantify their needs. How often are they likely to use your services, and how much revenue might you expect in the first quarter and first year? Can you further entice them with a volume discount arrangement?

If you start your company with contracted work in hand, you have a much greater chance of building your business in the critical first three years. Your presold customers are those most likely to repeat, since they anticipated their need ahead of time and know it's likely to be recurring. That softens some of the pressure to sell while you concentrate on getting operations running smoothly.

This first baby-steps foray into selling might feel uncomfortable, but once it's done, you'll have gained a lot more confidence. Don't let your discomfort lead to procrastination. A good friend, a sales professional, helped me with this mental block. "Jeff, think of it like going to the driving range and hitting a bucket of balls. You'll tee up a lot of bad shots, but you'll get better. Start talking about what you do, at networking events and trade shows, where the stakes are low. Hit a bunch of those range balls, and you'll be better prepared for the higher-stakes conversations."

For a long time, we were pricing too low, out of fear—telling ourselves the customer would be alarmed if we charged more. I was still afraid to raise my prices even after ten years of successful sales!

I have several very good friends—trusted advisers—who built successful businesses themselves. One said, "You have a high-value niche product—stop being afraid to charge for the value it brings to the customer. Do the experiment, raise your prices until they say no, and discover the real value."

I trusted his advice and gathered the courage to act on it. Raising prices wasn't easy, but we didn't lose a customer. I wish I'd known how to value our product earlier!

Dr. Joseph Simpkins

Founder, Virscidian Inc.

TIMING YOUR JUMP

In the best-case startup scenario, you continue to receive a paycheck and company benefits from your employer while in the planning stages for your business. Almost everyone who voluntarily leaves a job, whether for a better fit or a new adventure, plans ahead—you should too. But unlike leaving for another post on someone else's payroll, making the big jump onto the entrepreneurial path often feels fraught or loaded. If you're leaving corporate employment for self-employment for the first time, the jump into the abyss can seem very exciting but very risky.

Let's talk about some of those pressures, real and imagined, so you can put them in better context with your situation and wisely choose your timing.

YOUR TIME IS LIMITED

If you're fulfilling a full-time commitment to your employer, you're putting in a roughly forty-hour week at your day job—with likely little thought or activity given to your budding startup. Meetings with bankers, advisers, or potential customers take place on vacation time, lunch hours, outside of work. If you have a family, that pulls time from your hours with them. This is not quite the same as spending evenings in an executive law degree or MBA program—those are finite and predictable commitments with a defined reward at the end. After trying to work your day job and on your startup for an extended time, you will ask yourself, *How much longer can I do both?*

YOUR STATUS IS AT RISK

Your colleagues, and maybe your boss, might find out what

you're planning. This may affect your job status. Why would the company think of promoting you or giving you a raise if you're not committed? Will your colleagues undermine you behind your back and spread rumors that you're not giving 100 percent? I won't lie to you—this happens. By trying to operate secretly, you may position yourself for unfair criticism.

It's possible your worries are inflated by a tendency to try to overmanage risks during startup. As you become sure of your upcoming departure, instead of planning covertly, consider openly discussing your business dream with key colleagues and even your boss, asking for their support and opinions. Such a conversation gives you a chance to make it clear you're a dedicated employee until your departure. You may even be able to position yourself as a likely contractor to your former firm after you get going.

INSURANCE AND OTHER BENEFITS ARE IMPORTANT

If your partner's employment can cover your family's health insurance benefits, great. If not, you need to have these benefits in place in your new company from the beginning. This is not always easy—salaries and benefits follow revenue, and revenue follows startup of operations. This can be a deal stopper for many budding entrepreneurs with families. If you're single with few obligations, the risk is not as dire.

You have options. In the United States, leaving a job that provides health coverage entitles you by law to self-paid continuation of some benefits, such as health insurance—known as the COBRA program. You get to continue the same healthcare plan you're already familiar with, but you have to pay for it. You can use some of your working capital or startup funds to cover this expense, but in most cases, you'll want to quickly earn revenue to cover family income and needs. Many entrepreneurs use their savings or home equity, but most try to limit spending or borrowing on personal assets unless there are no other options. If you choose to self-fund your operation, you will feel even more pressure to speed up revenue.

YOU'RE NOT GETTING ANY YOUNGER

It takes years to accumulate your level of training and expertise, and positioning yourself to start your first company can take many more. I was forty years of age when I started my first operation, and forty-eight when I started my most successful one. You may notice younger entrepreneurs seem energetic and charismatic, especially when they receive the inevitable press coverage. You may feel discouragement when you see "30 under 30" and "40 under 40" articles in your local business or trade journal. It can feel like you missed the boat when it comes to business, that your entrepreneurial ship has sailed. Ever wonder why there aren't any "50 over 50" or "60 over 60" pieces?

You might also encounter silver-haired gentlemen wearing bespoke suits and Patek Philippe watches who found companies for a living. I've met these "entrepreneurs" and heard some claim to have founded forty, even eighty, companies. I've listened to them prognosticate at conferences where they always seem to be keynote speakers. They are intimidating. You may feel inadequate for the task ahead of you. You might think, *What do I know compared to their experience?*

Listen, these are head games we play with ourselves—the self-doubts playing on endless loops, a sense that we don't belong, false beliefs that we don't deserve success, or feeling that we're fakes. This negative self-talk loop is referred to as impostor syndrome, but I usually just call it "head trash." Mindset is critical—it takes mental focus to believe in yourself. Self-assuredness does not come easily every day, and it must be practiced. We'll explore more about mindset as we push into the chapters on sales and sales skills. For now, consider whether your self-doubts or self-perception are influencing your timing for quitting your day job.

KEY TAKEAWAYS FROM CHAPTER 2

- It's worth thinking (and writing down) some thoughts about mission, values, vision, and purpose. The fact that some big corporations pay only lip service to the human part of a business does not mean these principles won't help you succeed.
- Your go-to-market strategy is more than an investor buzz phrase. You'll refine your strategy over time, but you must start thinking, before you start up, about how your company will earn revenue and profits.
- Operations is what you already know how to do. Trust that you can do that well, but learn how to *sell*.

CHAPTER 3

SETTING UP YOUR COMPANY

We've covered much of the *thinking* you should do before you start operations. The following sections cover some of the important *infrastructure* you should have in place before doing business with customers.

BUSINESS STRUCTURE

When you start a business, you will need a dedicated bank account. To do that you'll need to get a federal employer identification number (FEIN), also called a tax identification number (TIN). To open your business account, banks also need to know what legal structure you're using—the type of business you have set up and registered with your state. Is it a sole proprietorship, a partnership, an LLC, or a corporation? If you haven't already done a detailed analysis, choosing your registered business type will take a little thought.

If you don't yet have an attorney or a tax accountant involved in your business setup, ask other business owners about their structures. Ask more than one—and ask why they chose it. If you feel unsure, consider seeking an opinion from an attorney or accountant, who might offer an opinion free of charge if they think of you as a prospective client.

If you already have a lawyer or an accountant, you may get a recommendation but not necessarily a clear or comprehensive picture. Some lawyers and accountants make their fees from being experts, while others seem to think it doesn't serve them well to help you too clearly understand their trade. If you feel like this is the case, find a legal professional or financial adviser you trust.

There are lots of opinions online about the advantages and disadvantages of the common structures. The website of the US Small Business Administration (SBA.gov) is a good place to start. I also recommend that you relax a bit. Think of your structure as a starting point. Unless you choose an advanced structure at the outset, such as a corporation filing taxes under subchapter C, commonly called a "C corp," it's typically not too difficult to restructure if your business growth demands it. I suggest that you do your own research, but here I give quick summaries of the business structures most frequently used by for-profit companies.

SOLE PROPRIETORSHIP

This is easy to understand. You're the company. You can get a TIN and a bank account, to separate your business revenue and expenses from personal, but on your tax return any money you make from the business is taxed as your personal income. It's a little more complicated to prepare your return, but you have too much responsibility as an owner to do your own tax filing anyway.

The problem with sole proprietorships is they do not shelter you from liability, so any and all of the business debt is yours. Also, if an employee, a customer, or a vendor were to sue you,

you'd be 100 percent liable for any judgment against the company. I recommend you consider a more robust structure that offers you some separation from your company, especially if you intend to hire anyone. I also highly recommend you level up from sole proprietor if you might work on projects under regulatory controls, since a mistake on your part could affect your customer's regulatory liability and come back to haunt you.

Single-person consulting firms sometimes set up sole proprietorships, particularly if the consultant does not work on projects that may affect future review by a regulatory authority such as the US Food and Drug Administration (FDA) or the Occupational Safety and Health Administration (OSHA). If you have already started up as a sole proprietor, it is not at all difficult to incorporate and restructure if you choose.

LIMITED LIABILITY PARTNERSHIP

A limited liability partnership (LLP) is occasionally useful for those who offer contract services. This structure requires that one managing or general partner share personal liability with the company in the event of a lawsuit. However, the other partners, silent or otherwise, enjoy limited liability—they are personally sheltered. This structure allows a founding partner to retain greater control, and more easily attract investors or partners, who take on less legal risk.

The LLP structure is most often used with companies like law firms and physician groups—in fact, some states require this structure for these firms. But the LLP is also a consideration if your company is, for example, a group consulting practice. Your accountant or attorney, when you have one, will advise you regarding insurance or reserves to sufficiently shelter you personally in the event of litigation.

LIMITED LIABILITY COMPANY

A limited liability company (LLC) is a very common structure for smaller companies with one or several owners. It offers *all* owners limited liability—personal shelter from company debt and lawsuits—plus the option to share profits either according to percentage of ownership or by agreement with the other owners or with members. Just as with the structures discussed above, an LLC is a "pass-through entity" in the tax code, meaning its profits pass directly to the owners to be taxed as personal income. Because all the profits are treated as personal income, the company does not pay your Medicare and Social Security taxes on those profits—you do.

Know that "limited liability" does not extend to any company obligation you cosign as an individual, and you may have to personally guarantee some company debt early on. It is very common, for example, to lease laboratory or other equipment, and until the company has sufficient financial strength to guarantee these obligations without you, the bank or leasing company will want your signature on the note. Limited liability does not extend to debt obligations you personally guarantee— if the company defaults, the banks will look to your assets to get their money.

LLCs are a great option at startup and in growth phase, but they have a couple of disadvantages that may be limiting as your company matures. It is more difficult to take on equity investors, or to sell your company, as an LLC, so if you have future plans that might involve investors or buyers, remember they prefer corporations. It is also impossible to make incentive stock grants to your employees, although there are workarounds you could explore, such as so-called "stock appreciation units," which give grantees rights to a share of the profits if the company is ever sold or otherwise liquidated.

In many states, an LLC can be fairly easily converted to an S corporation or C corporation (both types are covered in more detail in the following sections). Their names come from tax code terms—as a corporation, you may choose to be taxed under subchapter S or subchapter C. Check your state's requirements prior to converting to this structure—many states allow you to transfer assets directly, but a few require that the LLC be dissolved and a separate corporation be formed. When you convert, an S corporation is often easier because it is also a pass-through entity, while a C corporation requires a restatement and restructuring of the company's accounting. Planning ahead minimizes costs, so if your goal is to convert to a corporation to make the company more attractive on the block, do it *before* you look for your buyer or investor!

C CORPORATION

Technically, this is a corporation that files its taxes under a specific set of tax rules. The primary difference is that corporate net income is taxed at corporate tax rates, and profits distributed to owners are taxed again. So, if your company is a corporation, you pay personal taxes on your salary, the company pays taxes on profits, and any remaining profits the owners elect to distribute are taxed again as dividends on your personal return. This is often called "double taxation," and avoiding it is a common reason for owners to choose a pass-through structure.

If your company is setting up a shop with expensive equipment, such as a lab, to develop products or provide services, it's likely you will operate for several years before making enough money to pay corporate income taxes. Tax breaks meant to encourage business growth, such as net operating loss carry-forwards (NOLs), mean operating losses as you get up to speed can offset your first years of profitability. Many companies pay no corporate taxes until they have been operating for five to ten years. Avoiding double taxation is not an issue in this case. Companies expecting to quickly turn large profits might gain more by using the LLC or S corporation structure.

The corporate structure is more complex than LLCs, LLPs, and sole proprietorships—bylaws, annual meetings, directors, officers, and the like, are required by law. You can often use document templates supplied by your attorney to make the required filings. The setup cost for a corporation is initially a bit higher, but it may save money and headaches later to set up this way at the outset, especially if your plan includes investors or a downstream sale.

S CORPORATION

Just as a C corporation files under a different set of rules, so does an S corporation. An S corp is a C corp with a different tax structure and a few more restrictions. S corps can have only up to one hundred investors, all of whom must be US citizens. The profits from an S corp are taxed as personal income to the owners according to their ownership share, and more owners (up to one hundred total) can be added later. An S corp can be converted to a C corp by simply filing to revoke its own selection of the S filing, and this is more common at this writing as corporate tax rates are presently quite a bit lower than personal tax rates. It is sometimes harder to attract investors to an S corp versus a C corp because institutions favor the C corp structure, and C corps offer more options to give management control of the terms of a later sale.

S corps are subject to the same requirements as C corps for a more defined structure and take about the same degree of effort to set up. Upon sale of the company, if the buyer is another company or otherwise not an individual, the corporation dissolves, and the transaction is usually a purchase of all assets rather than a stock purchase. It's too much to get into here, but there can be negative tax consequences for the sellers compared with selling a C corp. For these reasons I strongly suggest consulting both an attorney and a tax accountant prior to choosing a structure.

B CORPORATION

The B corp is a newer entity that must specify both a mission and a profit purpose. These are becoming more popular as people all over the country have begun to consider whether corporations could or should have responsibilities to their communities or to the environment. To certify your company as a B corp with your state, you need to conform to strict guidelines in defining your purpose, be certified by a qualified agency (for which you will pay a fee), and annually file reporting documents with the state.

Consider a B corp if you, like others, believe in a greater good. As there is nothing about structuring a B corp that differs from building any other successful company *except* how you realize your returns from the business, we won't further delve into this topic.

Online services that offer simple corporate setup for a fee are fast, easy, and affordable, and they save you the struggle of finding an attorney and paying a retainer to get started. The corporate documentation these sites provide, however, is rudimentary. As your business grows, if you begin to see the need for more robust legal framework—say, because you think you may acquire a company, merge, or be acquired at some point—I strongly suggest you hire an attorney to develop and file solid corporate documents for you and your company.

I can't make a specific recommendation for your company without knowing more about what you intend to do, but these are some general questions I would ask before offering my opinion:

- Will you be hiring employees?
- Do you have partners? Are they working or silent?
- Do you have investors? Do you plan to look for investors in the future?
- Are you planning a growth strategy, or just looking to build up income and live comfortably?
- Will you eventually sell to family, employees, or another company?
- Do you dream of your company contributing to your community?
- Will you buy or lease equipment (beyond office equipment and personal computers)?
- When does your financial modeling show profit earnings?

If you don't immediately know the answers, don't worry. But consider each question for a few minutes, and visualize the different scenarios each suggests. What will your company look like in three to five years if you pursue different options suggested here?

INSURANCE AND ATTORNEYS

Everyone's favorite subjects, right? As much as I like working with my insurance broker and my attorney, I have to say that these essential supporters of my business are experts in fields that consistently make my eyes glaze over (and maybe they feel the same about my science-y stuff). The only reason I don't lump my accountant in with them is that I've become pretty good over the years at using my understanding of accounting to my advantage, and that has kept me more engaged. For legal and insurance work, I prefer to just trust the experts.

That said, some very basic understanding will help you decide what support you need—and what you don't—from your insurance broker and lawyer.

Business insurance is essential to protect you from potentially losing everything. It's also required in order to do business in many situations. If you lease a facility or vehicle, you probably need to name your lessor on your insurance policy and provide them with a "certificate of insurance" (your broker processes these for clients every day). If you sign a services agreement with a client, they may require you to specify—and in a few cases even want proof—that you have insurance at specific limits. I suggest telling such clients what your coverage is and asking if that will be sufficient, rather than raising your limits in response to what might be written in their standard services agreement. Remember, in business, many terms and conditions are negotiable.

These are several common insurance policies for the types of companies discussed in this book.

- **Business property insurance** offers coverage in case of loss of essential equipment, as in a fire or flood. If you have a lot of equipment in a multitenant building, a loss could be the fault of another tenant or the landlord. That doesn't matter to you—get your own business property insurance, and let the insurance companies deal with blame. The cost of your insurance premium is dependent on the value of your equipment.
- **Business interruption policies** cover your expenses and loss

of revenue for the period that it might take you to get up and running again after a disaster. Remember that you will still have expenses and no revenue to meet them.

- **General liability** is likely familiar to your home or auto policy—in essence, it covers claims made by outsiders (maybe customers) who are injured on company property or through doing business with you. General liability coverage is usually legally required and has limits. A $1 million limit is good base coverage for doing business in technical fields. You'll often see this quoted like this, for example: *$1 million to $2 million commercial general liability*. That means you're covered for up to two claims in a year of your maximum $1 million coverage.

- **Workers' compensation** (often called "workers' comp") coverage provides wage replacement and medical benefits to employees injured in the course of employment. It is mandatory coverage in most states. The benefit to the employer is that the employee does not have the right to sue the employer for negligence.

- **Commercial auto insurance** covers you and your employees for auto accidents while using vehicles for business. It is not the same as personal auto insurance, and should be considered if you or your employees must use their vehicles or company vehicles frequently for business, e.g., making deliveries. Your agent can tell you what's appropriate for your business.

- **Professional liability**, also called "errors and omissions," or E&O insurance, provides coverage if someone claims they incurred damages due to your company's negligence or violation of regulations. If your customer relies on you to produce work that will be scrutinized by the FDA or any outside agency for compliance with regulatory guidance or law, you probably need professional liability insurance.

Those are the basic business insurance coverages. Other than professional liability, which only some businesses need—buying it may be a judgment call for you—the other coverages are standard for a company that has a facility, employees, and equipment. You may find that some insurance underwriters will work with you only if you are in certain industries. For some reason (I've never gotten a clear answer), my industry—pharmaceuticals—is one that only a few insurance providers will cover. You may also run into limited choices if you work with energy, chemistry, pathogens, or animals. Keep shopping—you will find a broker that can help.

Lawyers are easier to acquire in some ways. I always find it's helpful to have an attorney on retainer—a few thousand dollars up front secures my position as a client and offers an incentive for them to become familiar with my business needs.

The following is a list, although not exhaustive, of several common scenarios in which corporate attorneys are helpful.

- **Corporate setup.** This includes legal structure, bylaws, shareholder agreements, compensation and employment agreements, and stock incentive plans. If you set up an LLC or corporation using an online service such as LegalZoom, you will receive some basic corporate documents and share certificates. These will not be sufficient should you have the opportunity in the future to expand or liquidate through a merger or acquisition. If either of the latter are in your future, consider hiring an attorney to handle the corporate setup.
- **Legal agreements.** Many in technical industries are compelled to put nondisclosure agreements (NDAs) and services agreements in place before starting any business discussions. This is because inventions in these areas are potentially valuable, so intellectual property is closely protected. You may

think executing an NDA before even having a conversation is overzealous, but, if you operate in this sphere, accept that you'll see a lot of these. Over time, you'll become so familiarized that you won't need your lawyer to review every agreement, but until then you can learn a lot by asking for a little help. A *good* lawyer teaches you what to look out for.

- **Disputes.** Many conflicts can be settled with a firm letter drafted by your attorney to describe your position. If a dispute can't be resolved so simply, your attorney should quickly suggest how to settle the situation.
- **Mergers and acquisitions.** Whether you're buying or selling, neither a merger nor an acquisition can be completed without a good attorney and accountant who preferably specialize in mergers and acquisitions (M&A). It is an advantage if your regular corporate attorney has M&A experience, but if not, they should be able to recommend to you the right professional.

As with any other supporting player you may need to work with over the long term, look for a good attorney. When I say "good," I refer not only to skill level, but also, most important, to whether they seem to care about you and the growth of your business. A good attorney also has ancillary experience (like M&A), a rock-solid reputation, a tendency to *not* nickel-and-dime you in billing, and so on. Your attorney is key to your growth as well as your profitable exit in the future. If your attorney enthusiastically supports your company's growth throughout your years in business, they will likely work hard to ensure you get the most profitable deal when the day comes for you to sell or retire. If they do, they deserve a piece of that profit in exchange for their long-term contribution to your enterprise.

ACCOUNTING

I do not teach accounting, although I've led some workshops on how to use accounting reports, as well as your accountant's skills and knowledge, to grow a business. You have already encountered some discussion of accounting in this book, and it will be touched on a little more. But accounting according to its standard practices is best left to specialized courses or books, which you can easily find.

Instead, I want to say a few words about what you need to set up in your business to keep your accounts in order. These are the basic functions to cover:

1. **Bank account.** In most states, you will need a commercial bank account unless you are a sole proprietor, and even then, it lends credibility to your business to have a business account. To open a commercial account, you need to have a company structure registered with the state in which you operate, and also a federal tax ID. Your bank will probably have a small business account option that can be expanded on later as your company grows. If your structure is sole proprietorship, your bank may call this a DBA account, which is short for "doing business as."

2. **Accounting software.** There are dozens of accounting software packages you can run. QuickBooks is a market leader for smaller companies, and newcomers like Xero are popular with very small or sole proprietor businesses. Some of these software applications were designed with specific types of businesses in mind, such as online retailers. If you intend to provide complex services via tailored proposals (configured around customer needs), and your invoices will be constructed with several line items, you'll do better to look a

bit above some of the entry-level packages. Online or cloud-based applications are great and getting better all the time.

3. **Invoicing and bill paying.** Retail sales are often by card or electronic transaction. Your service or supply business is more likely to send invoices to other businesses. You can do this with your checkbook or an online payment system like PayPal, or you can purchase these functions as part of your accounting software package—although they may be an upgrade from the entry level of the software. With PayPal and other online applications, you can also accept credit card transactions without any complicated setup on your part. Making these functions as simple as possible for customers has value, but they should also be easy for you. Otherwise, procrastination might happen more easily, and your cash flow could suffer. Also, if you must do your own invoicing and bill paying, you'll want them to take as little time as possible so you can focus on the high-value tasks in your business.

4. **Bookkeeping.** The function of a bookkeeper is to keep the business owner informed. At minimum, you should track your income statement and balance sheet monthly. A competent bookkeeper can get you month-by-month financial statements no later than the fifteenth of the month, current through the month before. We'll look later at what numbers you might track, but if you're waiting until the end-of-year tax preparation cycle to look at your books, you are losing line of sight as you try to steer your ship. A bookkeeper can be an internal part-time function, or you can hire a bookkeeping service. I guarantee the cost is less than the cost of spending your valuable time doing your own bookkeeping.

5. **Tax accounting.** You can use your personal tax accountant if they have experience working with corporate filings like

yours. If you're structured as an LLC or other pass-through entity, it's to your advantage to use the same accountant for both personal and business tax affairs. Corporate tax accounting is somewhat specialized, and unless you're a sole proprietor with some experience in tax preparation, this job is best left to a pro. A tax accountant can also advise you on the tax implications to you in transactions like partnerships, risk-sharing deals, mergers, acquisitions, transitions, and estate planning. Do not make your accountant your bookkeeper, or vice versa. Accountants are too expensive for bookkeeping, and bookkeepers are rarely tax professionals. You may find an accountant who has bookkeeping services in-house, and this may be worth considering.

Some budding business owners wait a little longer to get accounting functions in place, but unless you're comfortable doing this yourself, don't put it off. Nothing will kill your business more surely than failing to bill customers and receive payments.

HUMAN RESOURCES

It's pretty easy to hire employees, assuming people are available. And it's pretty easy to fire them, too. But it is crucial to do these things in a way that protects you and your company from liability and unnecessary costs. The hidden traps lie in compliance with regulations, both federal and state—and each state has different rules. Further complicating matters is that which state's rules apply depends on where each employee lives, not on your office or business location.

I address human resources processes in greater depth in the chapter on operations. At this early stage, the most important thing to consider is whether you're going to take on human resources (HR) functions yourself or use outside resources. You have basically three options:

1. You could learn the basics and probably be OK. This is less complicated if, for example, you work in the middle of a large state and have no employees in other regions, such as field sales representatives or regional managers. If you're in Austin, Texas, it's unlikely your day-to-day staffers live in Oklahoma or New Mexico. Find out what basic documentation you need to maintain on each hire, learn good workplace practices on setting policies and procedures, put together an employee handbook, and keep a locked file cabinet for everyone's employment info. Learn how to fire properly—meaning, make sure you are not violating employment laws or unnecessarily exposing yourself to an accusation of discriminatory employment practices. If you can employ "at will" in your state (meaning simply that you as the employer have the right to hire and fire for any reason), you'll be able to terminate but will have some obligation to cover your state's unemployment payments. If you terminate someone "for cause," which eliminates their ability to collect unemployment payments, you must meticulously document the cause. In any firing, clearly documenting the reasons in detail will benefit you.

2. Many smaller companies employ an HR consultant, usually on a retainer basis. Thoroughly vet this person, as the degree of knowledge and experience in human resources can vary widely. If you're going to commit to this arrangement, you'll want an HR professional who has broad-based experience to shield you from liability in every situation short of a lawsuit.

3. You can contract a suite of back-office needs—payroll, ben-

efits, and HR—to a professional employer organization, or PEO. PEOs are outsource-bundled services firms that serve employers for a monthly fee. Often you save money by bundling payroll with other services, and PEOs offer savings to their clients by giving small- to medium-size employers group buying power for employee benefits and insurance. But, like any company offering a very broad suite of services, you may find that their expertise in a complex HR field like employment law is not as high-level as you need.

Why might you need more complex HR services? Because employment law in many states is designed to protect large companies, not small or midsize enterprises. In the case of a small company involved in an employment dispute or litigation, it often seems the law favors the employee over the employer. In lawsuits brought against employers by former employees, I have seen settlements run into hundreds of thousands of dollars. Sometimes these are cases in which employees were fired for what seemed obvious causes—like disappearing from work for a month, or sexually harassing coworkers. An employer I know had to settle a wrongful termination suit for more than $100,000 after firing a worker who defecated in the owner's office.

These settlements are often necessary, because employment law is complex, termination procedures are hard to follow consistently, options are readily available for fired employees to claim discrimination, and—honestly—fighting a lawsuit is usually more expensive than settling. Setting up your HR function with forethought and a consistent, documented process can go a long way in protecting you from unnecessary litigation.

ADVISERS

There are three types of advisers—free, paid, and board members. This section is presented early in this book because founders often wonder whether or not they should have a board of advisers or directors, how to set up such a board, how to best use it to the advantage of the business, and so on. Also, as a founder you may find business and management consultants lobbying you for retained services contracts to act as advisers. A quick orientation at this point might be helpful.

Free advisers are simply people you know—or people introduced to you by people you know—who are willing to take a little time to answer your questions. Search for people with an experience base similar to your current endeavor, such as starting contract services operations, financing startups, or hiring talent. Ask for referrals and recommendations of people who might help with upcoming issues, and for introductions to lawyers, accountants, payroll firms, trade organizations, and conference organizers. You must ask them directly for their time and willingness to answer "dumb" questions, and thank them profusely afterward.

Most people love to be asked about their experiences and will happily help you. After you become successful, younger or less experienced people in your field might come to you for advice. You'll feel pretty darn proud to be able to pass along a little of your hard-earned knowledge to someone just starting out.

You can easily learn enough from the right free advisers to get you past the startup phase. If you're not sitting on a giant pool of money, this is the ideal way to go. It takes some effort to put together a good network, and to discover who can really offer help in your situation. It also requires you to be somewhat vulnerable, in that you'll have to admit to how little you know.

Get used to it. This is a good habit that will serve you well in lots of areas of life.

Paid advisers should be chosen after careful vetting and interviewing. Unlike a contracted job, in which you pay someone to complete the job for an agreed-upon fee, a good paid adviser will be with you for some time, working with you to achieve transitional steps along the way. Perhaps you need to build out a sales team or work on enhancing your company's value to sell your business in the future. Sometimes a corporate attorney or an accountant also acts as an adviser, depending on their capability and your needs. Before you interview a paid adviser, consider what role you would like the individual to play as you grow your company.

A *board of directors* is most often associated with investor-backed companies or those that plan to quickly develop value for shareholders. The board's role is to watch over management for shareholders, and the board usually has sole authority to hire or fire a CEO. If you are starting out with a small group (maybe just you) of shareholders who are actively managing your company, you do not need a board of directors. As you begin to look for outside capital, you can revisit the subject of forming a board of directors. Board members meet regularly and are often paid for their involvement.

Another type of board is known as a board of advisers or an *advisory board*. This group is usually comprised of recognized industry experts. By their willingness to associate their names and faces with you and your company, they implicitly endorse your business and lend credibility to your discussions with customers, partners, and investors. They may meet, or they may put themselves on an on-call status arrangement with you in case you need their strategic help. They are usually paid some sort of honorarium. A board of advisers is often an unnecessary expense—unless your plans to penetrate the market depend on the endorsement of these authorities. Advisory boards are most common to companies that are developing a new product and want expert backing to gain rapid recognition and credibility with investors.

Many times, the best way I can advise a new business owner during the startup phase is to say, "You don't need to worry about that yet." There are hundreds of considerable factors that will compete for your attention, and prioritizing which to address next is often hard. The feeling that you might be missing something critical induces fear, and fear often leads to stagnation or procrastination.

INFORMATION TECHNOLOGY

Information technology, or IT, is complex, demanding, and necessary to build a company. You need to send email, work on the web, back up computers and data, and make phone calls. Every piece of hardware or application will need to work together, or at least not clash. Whether your IT works properly depends on your keeping everything updated to current software and firmware versions. At various points, each purchase will become outdated or incompatible with a modern function, and you'll need to upgrade.

Fortunately, unlike in many other aspects of life and business, the necessary technology is becoming more simplified.

For my first company, we bought an expensive PBX (private bank exchange) phone system and a large bank of trunk lines from the phone company. These were wired together in a data closet with a couple of expensive networking boxes and fed through the walls and ceilings to offices. Alongside these were fed internet cables for network connection, again back to an expensive box in the data closet that hooked up to our dedicated internet connection. As time passed, our internet went to wireless connections through a single box, and our phones went to voice over internet protocol (VoIP). Then we transitioned to cell phones and only a single landline for the whole company, and that was just so the phone company would sell us the broadband service.

Over the years, we accumulated several boxes of communications gear—phones, firewall boxes, switching boxes, routing devices, mounting racks—that seemed too expensive to throw away. If you tour a facility while looking for a place to lease for your growing company, you'll often see a now-dark data closet with big boxes on a rack and cables running every which way that no longer lead to anything.

Today, you can get the basic functionality needed to run a business through a broadband connection, a wireless router, and an application that integrates your employees' cell phones with a voice mail–driven system. You're familiar with these: "For sales, press one...for service, press two...to reach a company directory, press zero...or you may dial your party's extension at any time." Almost anyone can set up this type of system.

Business communication has changed even more drastically since the onset of the COVID-19 pandemic, when so many people leveraged tools for working remotely, and application developers responded with increasingly better ways to keep the workforce working. Many companies used to buy computers for employees. Now, as cloud applications allow us to coordinate efforts without storing and exchanging files and data, many workers prefer to use their own machines when working from home. All that's really needed in the office is a strong and secure broadband connection, and oversight of our links to one another and our data security. The role of IT has changed again.

So, IT is one of those areas for which my answer is often, "You don't need to worry about that yet." The following are some situations in which engaging outside IT support may be helpful, and if any apply, you might consider contracting with a local provider. Otherwise, wait.

- You may have instruments or data collection systems that require off-site backup to comply with standards required by your customers.
- You may be running a laboratory information management system (LIMS) that requires integrity checking and frequent updates.
- You may have several generations of computers that run different operating systems, and staying current with patches and updates is cumbersome.
- You may have remote employees who need to be able to call for support if their computers have issues or cannot access one another or your server.

KEY TAKEAWAYS FROM CHAPTER 3

- Setting up a company requires you to do a lot of things, most of which get done once and are rarely revisited. It's worth considering what is urgent and what can wait—many times you can get started first and fill in unfinished tasks later.
- When setting up corporate structure, factor in your long-term plans for the business. It's not worth shopping for the least expensive option if you will have to spend time and effort later to get things done right.
- Technology will change and you may find your early infrastructure investment is no longer needed. This happened to many companies when applications from email to account-

ing changed from requiring internal corporate servers to being delivered by a "software as a service" (SaaS) model. Don't sweat it if your phone system is obsolete in five years, but try to spend less at the beginning on equipment to run the company, as opposed to equipment that helps you deliver your product to your customer.

CHAPTER 4

THE TRUTH ABOUT BUSINESS PLANS

Many entrepreneurs look for help from their local Small Business Development Centers (offices run by the US Small Business Administration), their local economic development corporation, and sometimes incubators or accelerators. The availability of such governmental or private resources varies from place to place, but entrepreneurs in many parts of the US can find some of these resources within a couple of hours' drive. Such resources have been around for years, offering access to advisers and experienced business leaders, sometimes through business boot camp programs, and sometimes with low-cost— or free—limited access via membership. Some advisers are generous, and others are passively marketing their assistance with the hope of future consulting engagements. The available resources vary, so if you have an SBDC office or a local EDC, reach out to investigate.

Through these resources, you can collect a mixed bag of advice. You will have to do your diligence to determine whether the advice is useful to you or not. Business boot camps are a great idea, but they are a one-size-fits-all approach to startup. You typically hear from an adviser (often an attorney) about corporate structure, an accountant about financial management, and so on. Whichever resource you use, at some point you will probably be directed to write a formal business plan. That's what this chapter is about.

Your program coordinator, or the retired banker advising you, will likely offer examples of business plans and templates. You can find templates online, too, and Microsoft Word offers a dozen or so business plan templates.

But what exactly is a business plan? At its simplest, it essentially says, "Here's a bunch of customers who need this, here's how we intend to address the need, here's how we intend to make sales, and in the end here's how that will translate to profits." So why do you need to develop a business plan, and how does it serve you? The idea that a business plan is a prerequisite for starting a company has somehow become gospel in the business advisory practice. I believe this is nonsense.

This formalism implies that all businesses, and their strategy at startup, are basically the same. It implies that you must do or know certain things—such as the size of your market and how much you will sell in each of your first three years—or you're not allowed to start. It ignores the fact that entrepreneurs take different paths to get started.

A *formal* business plan is required only by investors and bankers—people with money you need for your business. Moreover, many who require a formal business plan usually don't read it. You might remember in the 1986 film *Back to School*, Rodney Dangerfield evaluates a report by feeling its weight in his hand: "Too light. It feels like about a C. Bulk it up and add a few multicolored graphs."

If you're raising money from anyone besides bankers and investors, you're better off with a short, compelling slide deck presentation and some realistic projections to back it up. Thinking further forward, if your reason for writing this bulky plan is to raise money, what will happen to your business plan once you get the check? That's right—the plan will end up in a binder on a shelf, only likely to be revisited if you go out for funding again. It certainly won't be a guiding document.

In this chapter we talk about what investors and bankers really want to see when you go to them for funding. We also talk about what a truly useful—useful to *you*—business plan might look like.

> At the time we founded, services companies like ours weren't of much interest to investors, so I wrote a short business plan and went to our bank to request a loan. I don't know that it made any difference, but in the end my husband was willing to put our house up as collateral. Thankfully, he believed in me and my capabilities to be willing to do this. I wouldn't have been able to do it without the loan—and his support.
>
> Dr. Judy Carmody
>
> Founder, Avatar Pharmaceutical Services and Carmody Quality Solutions

WHO IS THE BUSINESS PLAN FOR?

People write a business plan most often because someone requires it of them. Drafting a comprehensive business plan can be a lot of work, and your time is pretty thin before and during startup. What do you *really* need to have planned at this point, and why?

If you follow the classic full business plan format, there are two parts that will consume a lot of your time, and the rest will sometimes feel like filling in packing material around these.

First, you'll spend a lot of time analyzing your market and developing a go-to-market strategy. However, as soon as you launch, you're going to learn a lot about how to better position your company, and you will likely change your marketing plans.

Second, a standard practice is to include in your business plan a set of *pro forma* financial statements—future period profit-and-loss statements and balance sheets that represent your prediction of how the company is expected to perform financially. Many founders simply aren't comfortable with developing their own financial statements and might instead opt for a long, painful, and potentially expensive conversation with their accountant. As a technical expert, you're probably not at all comfortable with looking months and years ahead, making predictions of revenue and profits based on no history at all. Doing so might feel like fabricating data, and we tend to have a strong internal prohibition against doing that!

These are the people who might ask for, or require, a full business plan from you:

1. **The person or group teaching your entrepreneurship class or workshop.** Because you stand to gain little from putting a lot into this assignment, use your judgment to determine the amount of effort you exert. Generally, little funding is made available in these classes—in fact, you probably had to pay an entry fee—but occasionally you'll see a "business plan competition" with a cash prize linked to these courses.

2. **Advisers you might connect with** through incubators, local economic development offices, the Small Business Administration, or the Service Corps of Retired Executives (SCORE). These advisers are often just following a formula, so try to understand why they see this as necessary. If you don't get a clear answer to explain the reason a business plan is being drafted, you might want to look for a different adviser.

3. **Investors who might want a business plan.** I often feel that investors in raw startups are following a formula that helps them disqualify unprepared candidates, so this request is

a bar you'll have to jump over just to get an opportunity to have a conversation. To know they have a reasonable chance of a return on their investment, investors need to see that you have your act together.

4. **A bank officer qualifying you for a commercial loan.** The bank's need for this is a formality—they are not looking for some validation that you know what you're doing, that you're taking most of the risk, or that you stand a good chance of paying back the loan. If you've guaranteed the loan with collateral, for example the equity in your home, there's no reason to provide a detailed business plan. If you're buying equipment, that's also collateral. Present documentation, perhaps some financials your accountant can prepare and a summary brief, and the bank lender should be satisfied.

5. **Vendors that lease equipment.** An option increasingly available through vendors is to lease your equipment piece by piece. You shouldn't have to supply anything other than your signature. A lender will need a more detailed business plan only if their repayment is somehow linked to your success or revenue growth, and this kind of lending is rare when you're just starting out. An example might be securing a loan by demonstrating that you have long-term contracts in place, or long-term receivables (money your customers have committed to pay in the future).

6. **You.** Planning is a good thing when embarking on a potentially costly new venture, so consider requiring a business plan for yourself. This book is designed to help with that. The format of a strategy or growth plan to serve you can be more free-form and should focus on areas you've identified in which having a strategy is important to your company. The final section in this chapter deals with this type of business plan.

We're left with a fairly simple picture. Because of the differing needs of those who require it, there is no typical or standard business plan that covers the topics shown in the table of contents below. The idea of a formulaic business plan is stubborn and old-school. For investors, you need a compelling presentation with documents to back it up—that's one type of business plan format. For yourself, consider a strategic plan for launching, providing services, and finding customers. All other requests for your business plan should be questioned.

> I didn't really write a business plan, I just had some customers and started operating. This set me up to make some not-so-great decisions.
>
> The owner of the company where I leased lab space saw my early success and said she wanted to come in as my partner. And the first vendor I approached also wanted to be a partner. I thought this was great—it validated my ideas and gave me what I thought would be a safety net. Being an optimist, I thought having partners would be great.
>
> Unfortunately, being an optimist is an entrepreneur trap. You always think you can make it work out, you keep trying, and you assume the best in everyone else.
>
> When the relationships didn't work out and we disagreed on how to grow the company, I had to buy them out. If I'd had a plan, I would have used it as a guide for how we structured partnerships, but I didn't set up any structure at all.
>
> Without clear operating agreements on how to navigate that up front, the buyout payouts set us back at least a couple of years. Lesson learned: have a plan, use your lawyer when you need them, and don't just think you can make everything work with good intentions!
>
> Dr. Robert Suto
>
> Founder and CEO, Xtal BioStructures

A BUSINESS PLAN FOR INVESTORS

If you're designing your business plan to help raise money, you must communicate some basic factors. The exact style of your presentation (including your pitch, slide decks, and collateral) can be tuned to the audience and—to some extent—your style. Your job is to convince your potential investor that you will create a sustainable, money-making business—and to give them a clear indication of how you intend to pay them back with some gains.

There are five general investor types, according to the type of return they want:

1. Business partners
2. Interest and dividend investors
3. Angel investors
4. Private equity investors
5. Venture investors

Business partners may come to you with a desire to invest, particularly if you have a strong idea, have a strong reputation, or have customers. Partners need to be vetted thoroughly to make sure they are a fit—with you, and with the type of company and culture you want to create.

Recognize that partners are not passive investors. They will behave like co-owners, usually even when they have a minority equity position, and if you don't get along, it will be difficult and possibly costly to extract yourself from the relationship. Talk to your lawyer and accountant before allowing partners into your business, and make sure their investment is sufficient to make it worth the trouble should things go wrong.

Interest and dividend investors acccpt shaies of revenue or profits as you grow. These are often friends and family members who invest. They want to help, they believe in you, and they may get an ego boost from being part of your success. They may be naive and not fully understand the risk of investing in a raw startup, so make it clear to them that they have a significant chance of losing everything they put in—at the same time, try not to kill their enthusiasm.

There are small investor funds that sometimes invest in businesses for a share of revenue, but these are most common for restaurants and retail industries.

Angel investors are groups of small investors who share risk by contributing to a fund from which investments are made. These are often retired executives with wealth and a desire to have a hand in business. They may be overjoyed to have a position on your board or a consulting role in your business. However, it may be difficult to find a group that can evaluate and appreciate the possibilities of a highly specialized technical business.

Angels may offer you a loan that is convertible to stock later, known as convertible debt. They hope to make money when you expand enough to take on a larger equity investor—at which point they often sell their interest to the larger investor at a higher value.

Private equity (PE) funds also represent pooled contributions of several or many investors. What differentiates PE from venture or angel investing is a strong focus on improving the profitability of a business so it increases in value and can be sold. PE groups are structured in many ways, but often they evaluate your company to predict its value based on spreadsheet calculations, so if you have no business history you are an unlikely candidate for PE funding. The exceptions to this might be if you have an executive team the PE group knows well, or a niche that fits particularly well with other companies in the group's portfolio.

Venture investors typically do not invest in services companies. The linear growth curve for services companies is less interesting to venture investors than a company developing a product that may take off and produce an exponential growth curve. Venture investors often say that every investment they make has a one-in-ten chance of paying off, but that tenth company will achieve the growth goal of the fund. If you are developing a truly new idea or product, and the path to commercial success involves a prediction of fast growth, it's likely you're already familiar with venture backing. If you are an expert putting together a consulting, contracting, supply, or sourcing company, you can probably ignore venture capital.

If you are working to find venture investors, you will likely need to bring on—ideally as a team member or partner, but possibly as an adviser—someone familiar with the process of raising capital. This person will often assume the role of CEO of your company. In pharma and biotech, very often the founding scientist becomes the chief scientific officer or head of research, removing themselves from the burden of business management. This may be exactly what you want. If so, this book will serve to help you better understand the structure and workings of the business side, making you a stronger player on the executive team.

Venture and PE funds are managing pools of money that comes from passive investors (wealthy individuals or companies). The legal structure of the fund stipulates a lifetime or an investment horizon at which time the fund will be liquidated and profits returned to the investors. Because first-time founders have an uncertain track record for achieving growth targets on a timeline, these groups may not be interested in looking at your proposal at all.

Your business plan and presentation, then, should be viewed as a proposal to small, noninstitutional investors—individuals or small groups—to invest a specific amount of funding in exchange for a promise of a return within a reasonable period. In addition to the basic research and validation of your ideas that describe your business, you need to know these three things: how much money you need, what specifically it will be used for, and how you plan to pay your investors back with an added return.

I will not go into depth on the subject of raising big capital, as it could easily swamp this book. If you want to raise big capital, you still have a lot to do before you find investors, and you will have to do a lot of it on your own. This book is especially for those entrepreneurs who have a lot to do on their own.

**TABLE OF CONTENTS FOR A
SAMPLE BUSINESS PLAN**

Confidentiality Statement or Agreement

I.   Executive Summary
II. Company Description
III. Products and Services
IV. Go-to-Market Strategy
    1. Competitive Analysis
    2. Marketing Strategy
    3. Marketing Expenses
    4. Pricing Strategy
    5. Distribution Channel Assessment
    6. Launch Plan
V.   Operational Plan
VI. Management and Organization
    1. Organization Chart
VII. Startup Expenses and Capitalization
VIII. Sources and Use of Funds
IX. Appendices (*Pro Forma* Financial Statements)

The table of contents of the sample business plan shows that, if all the sections are well researched and thought through, it can convince a potential investor that you've done your homework to start a profitable business. It will show you know the following:

- Who your ideal customer prospect is
- How many prospective customers there are
- How you can access potential customers
- Who your direct competitors are
- How you will differentiate from competitors
- How you will price services or products
- How you will produce services or products

All of these are necessary to construct a realistic model of revenues and expenses that will convince your investors your business will indeed be profitable and to predict when that's likely to happen.

When starting a business, you may need to have a place to operate, some equipment and suppliers in place, and some early employees so you can produce, send invoices, and handle money when it comes in. You must cover the costs to get operations going in order to make money. Remember, you may need several people, plus a store of supplies and equipment and a place to put it all, before you can even send a bill, and that first check will not likely cover all that startup expense. The time it takes to receive sufficient revenue to cover your costs is called "break-even time." All the money you spend up to that point must come from you, lenders, or investors.

Once you have a model that defines your needs, further extend it to show what you will return to investors when you exceed the break-even threshold. How long will it be before you return their funds? If they have equity in your company, they will want you to increase your profitability because that's how your business will be valued when they exit their position.

The sale of your company is covered in more detail later in the book, but for now recognize that a significant investor, a merger, or a buyout may be the exit event your investors are hoping for. Often, agreements with investors will define the investor return at such a "liquidity event." If this is your strategy from the beginning—to eventually exit the business through a buyout—your predictions of future profitability and market trends in your industry will help you estimate when an exit is possible and how lucrative it might be.

Will you pay investors over time with a share of revenues or profits? How will you structure their premium, their return for tying up their money with you for months or years? If this is the deal you're making with them, be sure your business plan shows growth in revenue or profits so investors can calculate a realistic return. This clarity of future vision—not what will happen, but what you intend to happen—is exactly what you need to communicate to your investors.

What else makes a good presentation to investors?

- In describing your business model, don't lean too heavily on the science and technology. Stress the need that you meet in the market, and your experience in identifying that need and meeting it.
- A short, compelling pitch and slide deck should describe your business, your value to your customer, how you'll gain and retain customers, and in rough terms how and when you'll profit and exit.
- If you have any intellectual property that helps define your competitive edge, include that, too, in your presentation.

- Discuss how you'll use the funding, in broad but specific strokes.
- Keep it short until they ask for more information—often investors listen to many proposals, and they usually impose an absolute time limit. It's rarely over ten to fifteen minutes, so plan to be concise.

All other relevant information should be available to the interested investor as part of a prospectus or business plan. Depending on your potential investor's level of sophistication, this may include a simple set of supplemental material such as your résumé and your *pro forma* financial statements, or it may be more involved. You will learn as you go, and investor groups often have lists of what they're looking for. You can make distribution of the extra material contingent upon the investor group's informal expression of interest, so you don't have to flood everyone you talk to with expensive printed packages. You can also include a brief confidentiality agreement if you're concerned they may circulate your idea to potential competitors. Such concerns are not usually of high importance, however, for services and supply companies.

In your presentation, don't oversell. But do communicate your personality, enthusiasm, and belief that your business will achieve what you say it will: "I really can't predict what will happen, but I believe I can achieve this." As a scientist or engineer trained in objective analysis, you may feel you should qualify your predictions of a profitable future. I know that this is selling, and it probably feels uncomfortable for you. Recognize, honor, and project your belief in yourself!

You are taking a tremendous step as the expert who realized an opportunity existed, analyzed it, and built a plan to create a business around it, and now you will see it through.

You believe, you are betting on yourself, and you know better than anyone why you're doing this. Remember to share your belief, not uncertainty.

A wise man once called selling "a transfer of enthusiasm." You're selling your great idea of a lifetime, and you must be enthusiastic to have developed this plan and proposal. Let that enthusiasm shine. Give your audience the opportunity to believe what you believe.

My first business was funded using my retirement savings and stock options my previous employer issued. With a three-year-old daughter and my son on the way, I had to succeed. I had to feed four people.

Each business I start has been started using my own capital, although once I had success, I was able to attract other shareholders and operators to invest. Still, I always want to have skin in the game, so to speak!

Dr. Shane Needham

Founder, Alturas Analytics

As a UK citizen, my US visa required me to set up a growth plan—hiring US workers, evolving only within our specified niche—and report on it every year. So I was forced to hold myself accountable to a written plan. But this is really the way I've always done things, so I would have written a business plan for me anyway.

And it's always been for growth. Early on we chose our clients for their long-term return to us. That's helped us visualize how to maximize value, with the idea that at some point in the future we'll exit. I suppose I wrote a business plan that would impress investors, but without investors in mind. It's a statutory requirement, but this is the way I would approach it myself, and it's informed everything we've done.

Laura Browne

CEO, Covalent Bonds

A BUSINESS PLAN FOR *YOU*

If you've decided at this point that you don't want to write a business plan just because a lecturer, an adviser, a family member, or a book author advised not to—and you feel you aren't likely to seek investors anyway—you might want to consider writing one for yourself.

A business plan written just for you has three big advantages: (1) It doesn't have to conform to anyone else's ideas or template, (2) it lays out a map you intend to use and will therefore be able to modify if things change, and (3) it greatly increases your chances of getting where you want to go.

What do you want to achieve, specifically? How will you know when you've achieved it, or measure its success? How long will it realistically take? What are the first steps, and the second, along the path to your end goal?

Define that goal, then set up and follow a strategy to get there. General Dwight Eisenhower famously said, "Plans are worthless, but planning is everything." What he meant was that sticking to the details of a careful plan often proves impossible, because situations always change around you. But if you have no plan, you won't make decisions conducive to your strategy— you'll just *react*.

Strategy is how you execute your plan. It is not the goal. Many people confuse goals and strategy, and as a result they keep changing plans every time a new idea pops up that looks promising to move toward the goal. Developing a plan is important, and executing your strategy is how you will succeed. Don't go to the trouble of making a business plan for yourself and then fail to use it as a guide.

Here's a list of questions you might ask yourself in the planning process. I've supplied a few hypothetical but realistic answers to get you started, but of course, do your own thinking!

QUESTIONS TO START PLANNING:

- What am I doing? *Building a profitable business around my expertise and experience.*
- What will it look like when it's becoming successful? *Hmm, a lab with a manager and some smart bench scientists who have good reputations; a group of consultants who have all the skills needed to get a cancer drug to the clinic; me with six clients who use me as a trusted adviser and consultant in my field.*
- How much demand is there for what I do? *Well, I asked ten representative customers a series of questions, and they said they need just that and would pay this amount of dollars per month to have someone do it.*
- How are prospective clients getting it done now?
- What will it cost me to set it up?
- What licensing, permitting, or compliance issues need to be in place?
- How will I get the money to fund this?
- How much gear and how many people will I need, and when?
- Who is representative of my best customer?
- How do I differentiate myself and communicate my values to customers?
- Can I create a process for identifying and keeping more of my best customers?
- Can I create a business that scales up (becomes more profitable as I acquire and deliver to more customers)?
- What are my big operating costs?
- How can I measure my success, at least over the coming year?

Our services startup was 100 percent funded by the three founders. We wrote the business plan for us.

Later, we secured additional capital through debt financing—partly from a bank, and as convertible debt from two of the founders. The bank saw we'd been operating on plan, and that gave us strength to land that financing.

We followed the sage advice of raising additional capital when we didn't need it. And this put us in a much more comfortable position when the recession began in 2008—knowing we had sufficient working capital to weather the storm. In the end, the additional capital was never triggered, because we continued to operate on plan and we came through the slowdown OK.

Dr. Michael Kouchakdjian

Founder, Blue Stream Laboratories

There is not one particular area you need to investigate before creating your plan. Sometimes you can establish a company for simple and obvious reasons. I had a ready-to-buy customer with a big enough spend to fund startup of my operations, and a reasonably clear idea that I could sell to more clients. It did not matter much if I made detailed calculations of my total market size. I had enough numbers to know I would be profitable quickly, and rough metrics to understand how to hit my targets.

Perhaps you can see that your competitors-to-be are swamped by rapid growth in a services market you can address. Perhaps you have a patent or new method that gives you an obvious and valuable competitive advantage. Perhaps the big company you're leaving has already committed to contracting work to you rather than hiring your replacement. All of these could be reasons to start now with an incomplete plan and develop a more detailed one later.

On the other hand, if you feel overwhelmed, don't know

where to start to address all that must be done, can't choose between opportunities, or don't know whether to hire staff and buy more equipment or just push what you have a little harder, then these might be signs that a plan is exactly what you need to get you moving forward. A business plan you make for *you* is a huge asset at times when you, as owner, don't exactly know your next move.

A good business plan that you make for yourself is a living document. It needs periodic review, tracking, input from your team as it grows, measurables to keep it on track, and so on. It is your guide, your execution framework, as long as you use it and keep it current.

KEY TAKEAWAYS FROM CHAPTER 4

- Formal business plans may be encouraged in your entrepreneurship classes or business books, but think about whether or not a full-on, formal business plan creates value for *you*.
- Investors and lenders have specific but different requirements when they ask for your business plan. Both want to know what you're predicting and that you've done your homework. Investors want some assurance of a profit, whereas lenders only need to know you'll make your loan payments.
- Think of how a business plan can be valuable for you, as a record of why you started a business and what you expect. If you make it a living document, it becomes a tool for goal and strategy setting well into the future of your company.

CHAPTER 5

MARKET RESEARCH

"There are known knowns. These are things we know that we know. There are known unknowns. That is to say, there are things that we know we don't know. But there are also unknown unknowns. There are things we don't know we don't know."

—DONALD RUMSFELD, FORMER US SECRETARY OF DEFENSE

As Donald Rumsfeld so eloquently stated, there are lots of things that are unknowable, even though we know a lot. This drives most scientists insane. Your investors or bankers want to see your income and profit predictions looking forward three years. Don't they know this is just guessing?

You know today's hot technology solution will be yesterday's news soon enough. How do you know your customers won't find a new or better solution? And if your target customer is working on XYZ technology and you can help, how do you know how many other potential customers are working on the same thing?

Market research involves educated guessing, predictions of the future, no major disruptive advances (fingers crossed), and numbers that are just plain hard to get. Market research companies produce reports that are hundreds of pages long with lots of colored charts and graphs (remember Rodney Dangerfield's character in *Back to School*). These reports can cost thousands of dollars, but a quick online survey of reviews of the companies who produce them shows a wide range of opinions about their value.

If you're working on market research to vet your company business plan, here are some tips to work from a more systematic—and appealing to scientists—approach.

COMPETITION

Understanding whether customers will buy services from you—and whether you can make a profit selling to them—depends largely on your competition. Here I introduce three factors to consider about competition:

1. If you have *little to no competition*, this may be a blessing or a curse.
2. If you have *lots of competition*, you must figure out a way to be different.
3. Your *competition is often not who you think* it is.

Let's pick these apart…

LITTLE TO NO COMPETITION

If you have little or no competition, there is a reason. Maybe you're one of the few people who can offer your product or service. It may be that you're an early bird, the first to think of offering this particular service. Perhaps others considered a similar business offering, and on analysis decided it wasn't sufficiently profitable.

If you're the first to the party, you may encounter an issue when you start to sell to customers—their lack of experience contracting for this service that no one else provides. This will likely lengthen your sales cycle (the time it takes you to go from prospect to paid invoice) and, again, it's costly to run any operation with no money coming in. If you are indeed the first to generate or foster an idea, the process of selling will likely include some compelling scientific presentations, perhaps at key conferences and certainly in front of prospective clients. Again, time is money, especially when you're burning it and not pulling more in. And attending those conferences has gotten to be so expensive!

Being first to market is better if you have an advantage that can be protected, like a patent or at minimum a trade secret such as a unique, hard-to-replicate methodology. These give your first-to-market status more value, not only to prospective customers but also potential investors. If you fall into this category, that may encourage you to take the path to investor capitalization, which eases the burden of a lengthy wait for revenue. A first-to-market edge allows you to charge top-tier pricing, which is what investors like to see. Even if it takes a while to get the first purchase order, bigger checks will translate to faster profitability, and the investors will get paid.

It may be that the barrier to entry in your space is very high—expensive equipment, time to develop a successful process, the requirement to be approved by a regulatory agency before startup, and so on. These represent costs to you and your competitors, who may have decided those costs are too steep.

For example, if you want to establish a lab to run a new type of clinical assay on blood samples, you have to get the equipment, contact suppliers, and even set up storage systems and validations. Then you may need certification from CLIA

(Clinical Laboratory Improvement Amendments) or an FDA inspection before you can tell customers you're ready to take samples. The operating costs before a business even gets to takeoff can be a big problem for a startup company.

LOTS OF COMPETITION

What if you have a lot of competition? The good news is that there's a validated market for your service, so the prospects you speak with know this service and how it benefits them. The bad news is that some competitors are probably already out-marketing you, and if you advance on their territory, they might steal or copycat whatever unique spin you do or have that's captured their customer's attention.

You may also face a present or recent price war as some competitors try to make the service a commodity. Maybe they've standardized or automated some phase in the process that allows them to underprice their competition, creating a "race to the bottom" among operators in the space.

If you analyze the market for your services and conclude you must price lower than everyone else to gain customers, you probably have a business idea that needs rethinking. You must find a way to differentiate—not by a glossier brochure or slicker website (or bargain prices), but by providing a unique service that offers more benefit to *some group of customers.*

You do not have to compete for *every* customer your competitors serve. If you can identify *some* customers who have a need that is in any way different from the standard market, you can create a customer base in that niche. Doing so successfully—making yourself the preferred provider for select customers—builds a reputation that will bring you more business in the future.

A simple pharmaceutical example might be evaluating new drugs by dosing rats. One purpose of this assay is to determine the "availability" of a drug by measuring drug levels in the rats' blood plasma over time. Now, if your company does this, you're competing with hundreds of others, many of them low-price offshore providers. Not so good. But if there is a need for specialization—like using *specially bred* rats that require non-standard lab skills and housing—to gain specific information in the experiments, then that's a possible niche to investigate.

COMPETITION IS...*WHO?*

Finally, although you might think your competitors are companies that offer services like yours, this is not always the case. In this book, you'll be asked repeatedly to think from the perspective of your customer, not from your own. From your customer's perspective, *anything that solves their problem, or makes the problem less urgent, is your competition.*

Think about this for a moment.

Famously, cosmetic dentists are careful not to put travel magazines in their waiting rooms, because a nervous customer might decide an island spa vacation will feel better than capping a couple of teeth.

Who or what else can command the attention of your potential customer? Perhaps you offer a software add-on that streamlines your customer's equipment calibration, which must be done daily in their warehouse. If a heating and air conditioning company stabilizes the warehouse environment so the calibration is needed only monthly, your solution no longer generates the same revenue.

To look at this from a new angle, you must know your customers and their typical problems very well. You are an expert in your field, so there's a good chance you have useful knowledge. Use it, *and use your network of suppliers and customers*, to conduct a thorough SWOT analysis. SWOT is an acronym for strengths, weaknesses, opportunities, and threats. There are many resources discussing how to do this, including lists of idea-generating questions and ways to brainstorm. For a great book on the topic, I'd recommend *The SWOT Analysis: Using Your Strength to Overcome Weaknesses, Using Opportunities to Overcome Threats* by Lawrence Fine.

My direction to you is to be brutally honest with yourself. Your ideas require thorough vetting, critiquing, and nitpicking for you to refine them into a solid plan with the best chance for success. Figure all the ways in which your competition—your real competition—can take business away from you. By doing so, you will discover the unique and exclusive way in which you provide value to your customer, and that will be the foundation on which you build your company.

You may feel uneasy asking others to critique your plans and your research, and to tell you if they believe you're right (or wrong) about your market. In recent years it has become popular to refer to critical vetting of ideas as "negative." "You're always so negative!" someone might say. Let me please reset to the past, when critical thinking was considered valuable. Any identification of a risk helps you make your idea better. Failure to identify a risk jeopardizes your investment of time, energy, and money. Critiquing a business plan may feel like you, or a trusted adviser, repeatedly shooting down your good ideas. It may feel like you'll end up with no way to move forward. This is not likely to happen. Your mind, fixed on the value of your idea, continually creates a better and better plan that in the end carries less risk.

The thing...is that you have to go all in. You have to believe, based on the information you have, that the market is there and the need is there. There's no halfway, no period of time when you can just coast.

That's great, very energizing, particularly if you have the support of your spouse and the people around you during the stressful times. But it's also really hard. There are always recession years when you're holding things together by a thread, just waiting for it to pass. You doubt all your assumptions.

We made it through the Great Recession because we had one client that was bringing more than 50 percent of our revenue. But that was risky too! We got dependent on that relationship, and of course everything eventually ends—we made it through the recession but had some tough times later when they transitioned out.

Dr. Robert Suto

Founder and CEO, Xtal BioStructures

TARGET MARKET

It's tempting to think you can provide services to all kinds of customers within a general focus. You might have a background in chemistry, with an expertise in scaling up chemical reactions to produce large amounts of a substance. You could contract with new drug developers, fine chemical companies, and flavor and fragrance industries. You might have expertise in structural steelwork that would allow you to take contracts from developers of any variety of projects worldwide. Why, there are probably lots of customers you could serve!

An expert in chemical analysis (like me) might also be open to working with lots of industries. I could even work in quality control or environmental analysis!

However, there are several problems with trying to do this:

- Selling into different industries means you must build a network and reputation in each.
- You will either have to tune your value proposition to reflect the needs in each industry, or pitch generic services—probably at a reduced profit margin, because only specialists come at premium prices.
- Your customers will not clearly understand you—are you a pharma specialist, or a paints and coatings specialist?
- If you don't represent yourself as an expert in one customer's segment, all customers might view you as less than expert.

You've probably heard the term "target market." Your target market is defined simply as the customers you are best suited to serve. You bring experience and expertise to the customer relationship, so you should define your target customers as those who get the most from you. If you select only customers who derive the most value from working with you, they will buy from you more frequently than those who get less from the relationship. Those select customers will pay more because they are paying as a function of the value they get from your service. You will be happier working for them, because we are all happiest when we know we're doing our best work and getting recognized for it. Customers will talk about how great you are, and that brings more customers. You will become stable and able to fire problematic customers, who soak up way too much effort and time for what they return to you.

Your business will grow faster if you direct your efforts at your target market. You'll put less effort and expense into sales and marketing, because your best customers will pay a premium, do more business, and recommend and refer you.

NARROW IS BETTER

The more broadly you position your company, trying to work with many customers instead of a select few, the worse you will perform in carrying out your business plan and hitting your projections. This is counterintuitive but nonetheless true. The most successful companies define their market—their ideal customers—very narrowly. As they grow, it may turn out they can in fact serve more than one type of ideal customer, but small businesses almost always start with only one subset. This helps you better communicate with customers and makes it easier to track the competition.

A friend is a business consultant who specializes in working with law firms of up to thirty staffers. He could, if he wanted to, work with just about any professional services firm, but by specializing he has become the go-to professional in his niche. Before specializing, he had trouble landing clients, but now his dance card is full. He's developed that go-to reputation so well that he gets calls from other firms: "I know you only work with lawyers, but we're an accounting firm that needs some help optimizing our business process. Can you help us? *Please?*"

When I started my analytical drug development firm, I chose to define my customer as "managers of oral drug development programs working from the preclinical to the early clinical development stage." As time went on, our company worked with later-stage drug development programs, developed some quality control assays, and stepped outside of working only on oral drugs (pills and capsules). We expanded *not* by offering new services or developing a new network of people outside our chosen focus. Instead, new types of customers came to us because they had heard we were doing great work for colleagues and acquaintances in other fields. Gradually, we developed a reputation for doing good work in new areas, and our prospect base grew and improved.

The more effort you put into defining your ideal customer, the clearer your marketing program will be, and the more you'll connect with clientele. Prospects typically don't trust providers who claim a broad range of capabilities, preferring that their important projects go to a specialist. If you try to compete with bigger, more established players by copying their lists of services, your prospects will wonder how you can do all that as a small player. Ever see a small company lead with, "We specialize in…" and then list ten services?

Go beyond describing your target market by industry. Think in terms of what drives them—why they will connect with you. Think about the expertise you gained in your field. Over time you formed beliefs about how to properly execute tasks, how things should be done. You have opinions and beliefs about the best way to perform your service or develop your product. Use that: try to find customers who share your way of thinking about your science.

A friend who owns a bicycle shop near my home, a couple of hours outside of New York City, has built part of his business around customers who escape the city for a quick dose of the country. He offers bikes and service in a rural location along a dedicated bicycle rail trail. His customers are looking for an experience, one of being immersed in a world so different from the city where they ride on quiet roads and bike trails past rolling farmland, lakes, and streams. His customer is a person who dreams of succeeding in a life outside of the city, maybe as an early retirement or in a weekend home.

Often-quoted business guru Simon Sinek says it best: "The goal is not to sell to people who need what you have; the goal is to sell to people who believe what you believe."

DEVELOPING A STRATEGY

In researching your target market and your competition, your strategy for building a customer base—for getting revenues started—will refine. If you do your research, and spend time thinking about what that research implies, you will begin to have "plan of attack" ideas. Let's talk about capturing those ideas in a structured fashion that contributes to your success.

You might realize, *I have so many great ideas now that I know more about competitors and target markets, and I can think of a dozen ways to connect with potential customers.* When your conscious mind applies a lot of time and energy thinking about the fundamentals, your superconscious mind starts to see relationships and generates ideas. These pop into your head even when you're not in market research mode—in the shower, as you're half dreaming in bed, at the gym. If you're one of those semimythical individuals who always carries a notebook and jots everything down, you may end up with hundreds of great ideas. If you're like the rest of us, you'll still capture a couple dozen of your best ideas. As the adage goes, "You can do anything, but you can't do everything."

Many people confuse strategy with goals: *I need a new pair of dress shoes for an interview; therefore, my strategy is to buy some new shoes. I will make a strategic shoe purpose today.* Hogwash! That's like saying, "I'm making a strategic choice to eat that doughnut."

The best-ever definition of *strategy* comes from Michael Porter, academic and business strategist, who said, "Strategy is choice. Strategy means saying no to certain kinds of things." What are you going to say no to, in order to say yes to something else instead? You can't indiscriminately pursue every idea that looks like it might move you toward your goal.

Strategy is execution. It is the process of executing a preplanned set of steps or tactics to reach a goal. The tactics are smallish steps for a reason, so if something changes, the tactics can be adjusted without throwing the entire plan into a tailspin. You will get further by sticking to the plan you made and adjusting as needed. That is your strategy.

As a business owner, founder, or leader you must allow idea creation to happen and then refine the ideas to craft strategic plans. Focus on where you are now—prestartup, maybe?—and where you want to be: *In a year I want to have at least $100,000 per month in revenue, an operations manager, and three junior scientists.* Evaluate your ideas and market assumptions, realistically based on their ability to get you to that ideal future state. Prioritize execution of your ideas based on your belief and your ability to carry them out. Pick out a near-term (I suggest ninety-day) set of objectives, making sure they're doable and measurable. And start.

Here's a basic template:

1. Long-term (three-year) goals
2. One-year goals
3. List of possible ways to achieve goals
4. Shortened and prioritized list
5. Ninety-day objectives
6. This week's actions
7. Start

Looking at your market in detail has the exciting side effect of drowning you in great ideas. Take a deep breath, write them down, and draw up one of your first strategic plans.

KEY TAKEAWAYS FROM CHAPTER 5

- Too little competition might be a warning sign that you've overlooked something. Too much competition in the market might mean the odds are stacked against you. Analyze before you start.
- Your competition isn't necessarily companies that mirror your services—it's anything that could entice your customer to spend money on something other than your solution to their problem.
- Tightly define your target market. Identify your ideal customer, the one who gets the most value out of working with you. Market to your ideal customers, and more will come.

CHAPTER 6

FACILITIES AND EQUIPMENT

Certain technical services companies face a special problem: the need to buy complex and expensive equipment in order to deliver their product. Many of us are trained to use highly specialized machines or software, and that training becomes part of the value we provide. We can't operate without having access to that equipment or those programs, which are very expensive.

I was told that it is impossible to bootstrap a laboratory company—meaning, to do it without some serious investors, or one of those venture-capital-backed pseudo-entrepreneurs. *Watch me*, I thought. I talked with four banks before I found the right lender, a smaller bank that was just developing its commercial lending portfolio. I had to sell my idea to them, boosted by my scientific pedigree and some letters of reference, and a good accountant and lawyer. I had to write a business plan detailed enough to impress them with its page count and jargon. And I had to use some personal assets, as well as borrow against the value of my new equipment, to get financing. But before I started, I had access to nearly $800,000 in capital.

If you're starting a contract services firm with a lab that needs some equipment, eight hundred thousand may be more than you need—or less. I was working with some expensive and touchy equipment, but I only needed enough to get us off the ground—later additions to the lab equipment would be easier to finance once revenue started flowing. I needed a laboratory, as opposed to a garage or basement space, and I wanted a working capital reserve of six months cash or so. You may be able to start smaller: maybe you can handle your first contracts working part time out of your basement, and perhaps you are able to get by for a while without employees.

This chapter addresses ways to buy or lease equipment you need now or in the future, and your options as to independent space for your company to live and operate. These are big expenditures, and once you commit you can't easily decide to quit and give everything back. We've already talked a little about preserving cash during your early days—let's look at how to handle these big expenses while being conservative with money.

> Ever since grad school, I knew I wanted to be part of startups. My first company was a startup. I was a minor player but a founding employee. I had a little stock, although when the company finally folded up, the venture guys got paid but there wasn't any real return for me. I learned that the venture capitalists' interests were not the same as mine!
>
> But I volunteered to help with the shutdown, and I got the opportunity to acquire some of the equipment. With no immediate job opportunities, I thought I'd open up a little shop with me and the instruments. I sublet a little lab space from a larger company, and I was ready to go.
>
> Dr. Robert Suto
>
> Founder and CEO, Xtal BioStructures

CAPITAL VERSUS EXPENSE

If your business is in consulting, you will likely work from home with a computer. You'll have some expenses, perhaps for marketing and technology tools such as videoconferencing applications, which are affordable and minimal. Even if you intend to build a group of consultants, each will probably have minimal startup costs.

Once you decide you need an office, a lab, or equipment, everything changes. Much of your startup time will be spent finding the right space and best prices, and lining up funds for it. Facilities costs may be somewhat flexible—we touch on some parameters below—but hardware is hardware, and it often has a high cost.

My last lab operation started in 2008 with new equipment valued at $450,000. It expanded six months later with an order for another $280,000 in equipment. Then there were supplies—everything from solvents and reagents to glassware and paper towels to safety glasses and gloves. These two categories—instruments (including equipment) and supplies—are often referred to as capital items and expense items. Capital items are used for a long time, and expense items are used once or only for a short time. As a simple example, if you run a shop that does oil changes for automobiles, your tools and equipment are capital items and the filters, oil, cleaning rags, and so on are considered expense. Capital items are part of the accumulating value of your business—your business assets—and expense items are not. Capital items have a few common characteristics:

1. **Capital items are used but not used up.** Capital items— buildings, vehicles, machinery, computers, and such—might eventually become less useful due to wear or obsolescence. But until they finally break for good or become run-down, they continue to serve the functions they did when they were new.
2. **Capital items are "written down" in value**, depreciating as

they age. The reduction in value year over year is determined in consort with your tax accountant. In my last company, we used a seven-year "straight line" depreciation equation, by which each item lost one-seventh of its initial value every tax year. This is important, because of the third common characteristic...

3. **Capital items are considered to be assets** of your business. Their purchase is funded by the business's income, maybe by making lease payments. While they are being paid for, the value of the assets is balanced against the remaining liabilities on their leases, and the difference is part of the value your business accumulates.

There are several ways in which your business might increase in value over time, and its asset base—the useful stuff accumulated by the business as it grows—is one of them. When your business does well, it pays you—either a salary or a distribution of profits. But remember, if it does well over time, it also becomes more valuable, adding to your wealth as the owner.

What is considered a capital item or an expense item is often pretty obvious, but some people get confused. Many items meet the description of capital equipment—they don't get used up, having practical lifetimes shorter than your depreciation period. Back when personal computers were newish devices, they were often useful for only about three years before the technology or software advanced to the point when a new one was needed just to keep everyone on the same operating system. Tax accountants tried using "short-term depreciation" and "long-term depreciation" schedules to deal with this, but I recommend you use just one schedule. A few purchases will end up dead before they are fully depreciated, particularly if you buy used equipment. Others will last longer.

If you're running a company that must be annually audited

for tax purposes, you might want to keep a list of capital items that are in service or out of service. But if you're early in your endeavor, your business probably isn't at that stage.

Perhaps the easiest way to think about capital items is to understand what one *isn't*. If you use it up, quickly or gradually, it's an expense item. Solvent levels in the bottle drop as the solvent is used, paper towels go from the dispenser to the trash bin, and gloves don't get stuffed back in the box after use. Expense items are accounted for as expenses on your financials statement, either in the cost of goods sold (COGS) section (if used to produce income) or in the operating expense section (if used to keep the business running).

You should also know that the value of a piece of capital equipment is what you paid for it—no more, no less. If you got a great deal from a vendor or bought it used, that's your cost basis. That is the initial value of what is called a "fixed asset" on your balance sheet. That's the value at which your capital item starts depreciating.

If you're not yet familiar with financial statements, some of this may be a little confusing. Later sections of this book offer clarity, and your accountant and bookkeeper can help as well.

USED VERSUS NEW

Funding is by far the biggest challenge for founders of certain services companies. By *certain services*, I mean those that require equipment or substantial inventory to deliver. Laboratory services, manufacturing services, specialized supplies or materials, and even stable storage and shipping often require substantial investments in gear. Given that, as discussed earlier, services companies are of limited interest to investors, getting started can be tough if you need equipment to begin operations.

Many companies look at used equipment to start up operations with a limited investment. This can be a very successful strategy, but with potential pitfalls. Here is a list of factors to watch for if you're considering used equipment for your initial or ongoing capital equipment needs.

1. Is the brand of the item well known and dominant? New models of equipment are introduced every year—manufacturers frequently develop new models in order to make improvements, add capabilities, and keep buyers' interest high. The dominant manufacturers have a much greater presence in used markets, so parts and service for old but still functional systems should still be readily available. When faced with a choice between a dominant vendor's well-used system and a minor vendor's alternative in newer or gently worn condition, consider availability of parts and support.

2. Is the equipment refurbished by the vendor or a creditable third party? If it's going to be used in a regulated setting, such as in an FDA-inspected operation, can the used equipment supplier handle installation and operational qualification for you?

3. A common strategy for financing equipment purchases is leasing—it helps limit large cash outlays, which can limit your available operating funds. Can the vendor offer access to easy leasing, or do you have to secure financing? Often, leasing systems individually is simpler than trying to obtain bank financing for all of your equipment. Lease agreements are often "lease to buy" contracts, meaning that after the lease term is up you own the equipment. In effect they are like a car loan—you're simply preserving your cash and buying the equipment over time.

4. Have you planned to stock parts, which are usually considered expense items and may be costly? Will you carry out maintenance and repairs yourself? If not, have you located someone who can fix the system if it breaks? Manufacturers often prefer to sell annual service contracts to buyers, but they won't do this if you buy from a third party. Paid service visits from the original manufacturer tend to be very expensive.

5. If you're stocking a lot of parts, it makes some sense as you expand operations to buy more of the same systems rather than set up your shop with gear from multiple manufacturers. Is sufficient used equipment from your chosen vendor available on the market to support your plans?

Finally, a cold fact of the used equipment market is that it tightens and loosens greatly with the fortunes of your industry. In the middle of the Great Recession from 2009 to 2012, many industries saw business closures, so the markets were flooded with used equipment. My company bought lab storage freezers for thirty dollars, entire suites of office furniture for two hundred bucks, nearly new scientific instruments (with retail values of $100,000!) for only eight grand. We picked up two brand-new drying ovens for regulated pharmaceutical manufacturing, free of charge, just for being willing to move them out of a facility. We sold those ovens two years later on eBay for $7,000 each.

As I write this, life sciences services companies in the United States are booming due to expansion in R&D services and lots of new investment in the sector. Used equipment is expensive and hard to source, so inventories of resellers and refurbishers are typically very low. In an environment like this, working with original equipment manufacturers to buy overstock or discontinued models—with vendor service contracts—might be a better bargain. Despite the likely extra cost, the lifetime of these systems is expected to be longer.

STRATEGIES FOR FINANCING

You've probably heard the phrase, "You've got to spend money to make money." If you're delivering services—beyond, say, your valuable advice—you will have to spend money to establish operations before you can deliver and get paid. Cash flow is important, but particularly in the early stages cash goes out to pay for whatever you need well before checks come in from satisfied customers.

Cash goes out to pay for three types of expenses: capital equipment; fixed costs like rent, utilities, and interest payments; and variable expenses, such as materials and supplies needed for delivering your services.

Capital equipment, as previously noted, becomes an asset owned by your company as soon as you acquire it. In accounting terms, it doesn't represent cash going out the door. You spend $100,000, and you own $100,000 in equipment. It's a conversion of cash to a possession, so the spent dollars end up as fixed assets. Of course, you did have to write a check or use credit (with its attendant obligation to write checks in the future) to acquire that thing. This ties up your future spending ability, limiting what you can do with the rest of the money in your account. But from the perspective of reaching break-even status for the company, capital expenditures don't count. What counts are the fixed and variable costs of running the business—once you can cover those with income, you've broken even. Until then, you're burning cash.

This quick discussion of negative cash flow during the

startup phase hopefully helps explain the need for financing and the complex calculation of how much you will need. During this phase, you have two objectives that may conflict with each other. The first is to reduce expenditures: hire only a minimum crew, buy only what you need, don't stock inventory, and try to operate in a small space. The second is to get off the ground as fast as possible so you can get paid. But obviously, if you spend too little, you'll get off to a slow start. Spend too much, and you're a fast-moving plane on a very short runway. It's your job to find a balance between the two.

Investor financing can cover your startup cash need, and investors usually understand the strategic balance. No investor wants you to run out of money, so estimate realistically and try to get funding on the high side of your estimate range. If you don't get investors, your options fall into three categories: self-financing, debt financing, and partner financing.

Self-financing is self-explanatory. Tap your savings, your home equity, your 401(k), even credit cards. Again, know how much you're likely to need and how much reserves you can tap. Even if you don't have enough to cover all of the anticipated expense, getting closer to the goal reduces the amount you need from investors or a bank loan. Don't underestimate the value that investors, banks, and even prospective customers place on your personal commitment to your business. A certain amount of commitment of your own resources is known as having "skin in the game," and you'll get more notice from others if you're risking your own wealth to do this.

Debt financing means you borrow. Borrowing to cover your capital equipment needs is relatively easy, because this is asset-based lending—the debt is "secured" by the value of the asset. In other words, if you default on a secured loan, the lender owns your stuff, and the value of that stuff may cover all or part of the debt. But debt that covers cash outflow during startup is "unsecured" and harder to come by. Because credit card debt is unsecured, credit card companies charge higher interest rates, administrative fees, and late fees. If you borrow your startup cash from a bank, you pay much higher fees and interest than for, say, an auto loan—which is secured, so the car can be repossessed for nonpayment. If you have a very good relationship with a lender and a good track record of paying your debts to them, they may take a risk on you. Contacting a bank you've never done business with will probably not get you anywhere.

Asset-based lending is different from leasing individual pieces of equipment. A lender will usually give you a percentage of the cost of the equipment you intend to buy, say 70 percent, in cash. Then you purchase the equipment using that money and other funds. It's similar to a mortgage loan. Leasing means the lender buys the equipment, and you pay for it over time with interest, receiving ownership of it when the lease term is up. Compare options—if you need to conserve cash during startup, leasing may be the better option even if the interest rate is higher. Your accountant treats either option the same—it's all debt financing.

An alternative to bank debt is a *promissory note* to an individual: a friend, family member, or other contact. Use your network—maybe someone close to you knows a high-net-worth individual who would back you. Some retired business owners like to help entrepreneurs. You may find someone who will share some of your risk by investing rather than simply lending to you. In Chapter 4, I offered some tips on what might interest investors and how to tell your story. Those pointers are useful in looking for private lending as well.

Finally, *partner funding* most frequently means customer funding. Depending on pricing and volume, you may be able to profitably presell services to a big customer at a discount.

In such a discussion, you commit to a start date and agree to how the products or services will be delivered. In exchange, the customer commits (for example) to a two-year discounted buy of your services with the first year paid up front.

This is more common than one might think. You may have read about young companies that made deals with bigger corporations for early or exclusive access to a hot product with big potential. Deals for services don't get the same press, but they happen frequently. The service provider usually doesn't want this information public, concerned it will create pressure from other customers who want similar discounts. The services buyer often doesn't want to expose the details of their business process to everyone else. Don't let the lack of press lead you to think these deals are unusual—if you have an interested prospect with cash and a significant need, propose a partnership as an option.

A less common source of partner funding is a vendor or supplier who finds a common interest in getting your company launched—someone anxious to expose a new product, for example. Usually, your small company offers little exposure to a vendor looking to gain an edge. Keep your eyes and ears open, though. You never know who might want to talk about—and facilitate—your great idea.

FACILITIES EXPENSES

If you can operate your company from your home office, garage, or basement, this section doesn't apply to you. If not, you need a facility, and it costs money to move in and start operations. When it comes to your facility, space, lab, shop, warehouse, or whatever you want to call it, you have two options: rent or buy. You might think that with the uncertainty of how a new business will develop, buying would be foolish. However, there are some sound financial reasons buying might be better for you, but in general renting is much more common among contract services startups.

To find suitable space, think about your development plans, the limitations they place on the type of facility, and timing. Think also about utilities, air capacity (if you have fume hoods, you'll need to deliver air to the space to make up for what's drawn out), floor and wall surfaces and their ease of cleaning, hot or cold spots, access (freight elevator, loading dock), parking for employees and customers, deliveries, possible tenant-shared spaces like reception areas and conference rooms, and ability to expand your footprint. You'll develop a clearer idea of what you value as you tour available spaces.

Find a commercial real estate broker, and start your relationship with a detailed conversation. If your broker knows companies in your market, they will likely ask sharp questions to help guide the search. The broker will work hard to find you space for as long as you seem interested. Most brokers prefer that you work with them exclusively, so you may want to interview several.

The broker gets paid by the landlord after you sign a contract agreeing to rent. This contract describes a lot of details beyond the base rent that are probably negotiable, like annual escalation, allowances for tenant improvements, and maintenance responsibilities. You may feel some pressure from the broker or landlord to quickly sign a lease to secure the space. Remember that both the landlord and the broker have a strong self-interest in closing the deal.

Do not sign a lease without your attorney reviewing it—and also have a detailed conversation about your plans and needs with the attorney.

Your negotiating ability on the details improves with a

longer-term lease, because the landlord will calculate their cost and amortize it into the lease term. This usually changes the rent by a small increment over a ten-year term (the preferred term for many commercial landlords) but is cost-prohibitive for the landlord in a short-term lease. That said, many landlords now specialize in short-term (one- to two-year) leases for startup companies. These property owners may refer to their buildings as business incubators or accelerators, which are increasingly available. This is particularly the case for IT and internet startups, and to a growing extent with lab-based operations. Landlords and developers have learned that similar companies have similar infrastructure needs, so it's not that difficult to fit a building with several smallish lab-ready spaces that share common utility systems.

Be sure to understand the rent structure in your lease. Base rent is usually expressed as dollars per square foot annually, so ten dollars per square foot for two thousand square feet translates to $20,000 in base rent over a year—divide by twelve to find your monthly base rent. Complicating the calculation is the fact that commercial rent is often charged as triple net (NNN), meaning net of insurance, taxes, and common area maintenance. The landlord charges a base rent plus a share of these other costs of operating the building. Before signing a triple-net lease, get an accurate value for monthly NNN.

Also get an estimate for utilities costs. These vary according to how the space is used. Fume hoods are a nightmare for landlords of multitenant buildings because, unless they were planned for the space, their draw may require the landlord to rebalance air handling across the building. If the landlord is unable to separately meter or control your space, you might have to pay a greater share per square foot for utilities than other tenants. If your heating and air are controlled separately for your space, you may run into a headache if you install heat-generating equipment or fume hoods, as the capacity planned for the space may not be enough for your needs.

If you intend to offer chemical or biological services, you may need local fire or environmental permits. Check with appropriate agencies for building requirements that could affect your ability to secure permits. Fire departments may place limits on what you can use or store, and environmental regulations may mandate treatment or containment systems on the building's main drain. In addition, understand up front how your use of the building space will affect your costs when you move out. For example, does the building owner or any agency have a decontamination requirement?

The last negotiable item, and an important one, is the tenant improvement (TI) allowance. This is unlikely to be part of a short-term lease, but in longer leases the landlord recognizes that you might have to build out the space to meet your needs. The landlord has the right to refuse any of your planned improvements, so describe these as completely as you can, but you will probably not have detailed plans prior to signing the lease. This discussion is about what the landlord will consider as acceptable improvements.

Landlords realize that many improvements, such as finished walls, carpeting, and window coverings, improve the value of the space. Other renovations needed for specialized activities might not increase the property value. The TI allowance offered by the landlord is partially or completely amortized in the rent using a calculated interest rate. For example, if you sign a ten-year lease at twelve dollars per square foot on five thousand square feet, you might negotiate $200,000 in TI allowance, but the landlord will raise the base rent by the amount necessary to cover the cost of the renovations, amortized and depreciated, over the ten-year term. So, the landlord is fronting you two hundred grand, charging you back all or part of the sum, and may get a return on the investment if your planned improvements increase the value of the building. If the rent increases only by $2.50 per square foot per month, you and the landlord are effectively splitting the cost of the improvements.

In the game of commercial leasing, you usually won't get this level of insight into the landlord's thought process. You'll get an offer of $14.50 per square foot for five thousand square feet with a $200,000 TI allowance. This makes the deal look very nice, and that's why it's quoted this way. *Wow*, you may think, *they're giving me two hundred grand to design the place I want, on top of everything!* Wouldn't you phrase it this way, too?

TI allowances are important for startups. Your landlord may suggest forgiving a certain number of months of rent if you pay construction costs for your improvements or changes. This might sound attractive—if you have $50,000 in contractor costs to pay, the landlord might offer to forgive $60,000 in rent. This is usually a bad idea for a startup—essentially, you're paying months of rent up front before you can even move into the finished space. Remember, your job is to conserve cash to give your business running room to begin bringing in revenue. Rent is a cash outflow, but it's a manageable one compared to the costs of building out your space before you can use it.

Don't assume a landlord will not negotiate just because they put some specific offer in the lease. A landlord will often forgive rent until the facility is move-in ready. You can sometimes negotiate months of free rent early in the lease, although some landlords will add the "forgiven" rent into later months. Also consider taking a larger space and subletting some to another company to offset your costs.

BUYING YOUR FACILITY

Another approach is to purchase a building for your business.

You may be thinking, *Wait a minute—my business isn't even up and running yet, let alone proven. Why would I invest in real estate to house it? That's a long commitment for something that might not survive beyond a couple of years!*

Yes, statistics show half of new businesses shut down within five years…or something similarly apocalyptic. It depends on whom you listen to, and whether or not we're in a recession. Either way, the odds aren't great.

There is a basic truth about real estate investing, too. Although it takes some work to understand the formula, and you must know something about the local market, real estate investing often makes money. You could argue that, just like buying a home versus renting, there is an equation, formula, or calculation that can sort the advantages and disadvantages of buying or renting your company facility.

Some big positives are in plain view—your control of the space means you can expand or contract your operation at will, depending on the occupancy of the rest of the building. You can pay your rent or not (or even pay extra rent), balancing the equity in ownership against the cash flow situation of your business. And, if you are in a local market where rents are rising, your equity will rise faster as well, providing you with a nice nest egg for your future retirement.

If you close your business, the building is still yours, and you can rent the space at prevailing local area prices. In essence, you are still in business, and your real estate venture may very well make money. Even better, you can buy more space than you need, divide it as appropriate, and rent the remainder to others. In ideal circumstances this can defray a large fraction of your facility costs, saving you cash during startup, and allowing you to reach profitability sooner.

In addition, if you sell your business in the future, the equity in the building is a fixed asset on your balance sheet.

I advised a business owner who ran a small (ten-person) architecture firm for fifteen years. She earned an income of $40,000 to $60,000 per year. She did not feel a sense of fulfillment, having made the entrepreneurial leap, especially knowing that architects with her level of experience were earning salaries two to three times that amount in large firms. In the end, discouraged, she liquidated her business and put her office condo up for sale. *Surprise!* The profit on the real estate sale was more than $1.2 million. This more than made up for her earnings gap. Instead of paying rent for fifteen years, she had been paying herself in equity.

The disadvantage most entrepreneurs face when making this choice is one of available cash. Commercial real estate usually limits the maximum mortgage at 70 percent loan-to-value, meaning 30 percent of the sale amount is required as a down payment for purchase of the property. This can be a big investment at a time when, as we've seen, you need cash for working capital during startup. Owners with money to do this are often older, and this introduces another term to the value equation—how long do you plan to hold the property before liquidating it as your retirement wealth? The value of doing this might look different at age forty-five than it does at sixty-two.

There is no single formula that works, and sometimes choosing the best path involves scenario-based thinking in addition to cold hard facts. Before deciding, talk to other owners and your accountant.

KEY TAKEAWAYS FROM CHAPTER 6

- If you're an expert in an equipment-intensive field, be prepared for heavy startup expenses. Consider ways to conserve cash—used equipment rather than new, financing rather than buying outright.
- Not all lending is created equal. For a startup business, leasing equipment best preserves cash but increases your monthly bills.
- Negotiating office or building leases is not easy, but it can be done. Ask your accountant and lawyer for help, and recognize that you don't have to settle for the offered lease or anything similar. Lease terms are negotiable, as many landlords are open to ideas that represent a win–win scenario.

CHAPTER 7

THE FIRST YEAR: STARTUP PHASE

Three major functions need to be coordinated in any business: (1) customers must be found, (2) customers must be served, and (3) the business itself must be maintained. The first is an external function, requiring the business to connect to the needs of the outside world. The other two are internal.

There's a three-way push–pull relationship related to the abovementioned functions: (1) if sales increase, (2) capacity to deliver must increase, which means (3) the business must reposition some of its assets (maybe using cash or simply extra hard work) to expand, buy better equipment, hire more staff, or increase efficiency. If the business moves too fast and spends too much, potential cash flow problems loom. Capacity to produce can be increased only when sales catch up. It's a beautiful cycle when everything is in motion!

These three functions are sometimes called "commercial" (sales and marketing), "operational" (day-to-day production and delivery), and "administrative" (business management, including financial aspects). Each function is crafted by planning and leadership, which might be just you, or you have partners or key team members. Although the push–pull means the three functions will work together and feed or constrain one another, each should be treated as its own process. As you build out your team, and the daily operations of the company become more complex, you will need an independent leader of each function.

We've been describing, listing, and rationalizing the steps and pieces that must be put into place to get your company started. Once started, you'll focus more and more on making the company run, and less on being its expert founder. As we talk about optimizing the business, I will apply the Four Value Signals concept (noted in the book's introduction) toward measuring the success of your efforts. The first of these is the team. Do you have the right people in place to lead and manage the three functions?

STANDARDIZED PROCESSES

As an expert in your field, you most likely have the deepest experience in running an efficient operation—you know how to do the work in such a way that it offers value to your customer. Things like training, operating procedures, task procedures, report formats, quality checks, and so on are all means by which operations are controlled and standardized. Using the same procedures to perform the same tasks over and over is efficient, and by standardizing, your staff gets good at doing them. They learn to work faster, with less waste, and they catch problems sooner and can self-correct. As a smart owner, you look for opportunities to improve, gaining greater efficiency without sacrificing value to the customer or quality standards.

If you understand this about the operations function, or process, you'll likely intuitively grasp that the other basic business processes also better serve their purpose if they are controlled and standardized. But doing this with sales or administration often seems harder to achieve.

Take finance and administration. Many might ask, "Aren't they just reactions to the situation in the rest of the business?" Yes, as a smart entrepreneur you monitor revenue and expenses, watching that you're on target and not overspending if sales are behind. But that's the art of running a business, right—reacting by making good decisions?

Wrong.

What about sales and marketing? If you hire good salespeople, who ideally have some experience in your industry, they will undoubtedly know how to sell to customers. If you hire people based on their track record, and train them in the products and services you offer, you should be all right. "After all," one might say, "the selling game is so personal, so based on building good relationships, that we can't really put a 'process' to it. You just have to get the right people and let them do their magic."

Wrong again.

In finance, the first big step toward creating a process is to monitor cash flow instead of revenue and expenses. Remember, your bookkeeper or accounting system should supply a trailing twelve-month income statement *every month* so you can track changes over time, and that's the beginning of understanding cash flow. A good way to mentally make this jump is to convert every annual expense to a monthly one—just divide by twelve. If you have a $12,000 insurance policy that invoices you annually every March, you already know you need to reserve money for this coming bill. Why not look at this as a $1,000 monthly expense? This "annuitizing" of once-yearly predictable expenses helps you embrace the reality that your business operates all the time, not just once a year. As a result of this shift in perspective, you'll push on other parts of your expenses to smooth out big fluctuations in revenue.

Here's a simple example. In a startup company, often the owner is the chief salesperson. But owners are busy, so they tend to push hard to fill up the capacity of operations and then effectively stop selling to focus on other responsibilities. They discover that this is a mistake after all the sold work is completed and no more sales opportunities are in the pipeline. Operations then start idling while the owner turns back toward closing deals. This unproductive cycling is easy to spot by monitoring cash flow. Annuitizing most expenses by month smooths out the noise in monthly financial reports, so owners can more easily spot the effect of inconsistent sales.

In some industries, fluctuations in sales and the need for investment in production happens on a predictable or seasonal cycle, so staff are hired as temporary workers or contractors, and they're terminated and then rehired (if available) when the workload fills up again. Good examples are fair-weather landscaping businesses, or retail sales that tend to increase during the holiday season. Business owners have an advantage if they plan their efforts around predictable cycles so their businesses run according to a system.

Monitoring financials for planning purposes means not only putting the books in the right format, but also reviewing them frequently—not just during the end-of-year tax filing. Smart owners monitor selected financials to understand how current goals and strategies are being met. By measuring and monitoring, you create an administrative process that invokes wise decisions based on data, rather than knee-jerk reactions when something breaks down.

SALES AND MARKETING

Treating sales as a process is also an important exercise for a business owner. A sales process starts with understanding clearly whom you want to sell your services to, and then creating a relationship that connects them to you when they are ready to consider what you offer. If you've identified an ideal customer profile, so you vividly know your target and what benefit you can bring to them, your job now is to invite them *at the right time* to do business with you.

Marketing is the process by which you make your company known to potential customers who have not heard of you yet. Because you want prospects to pick up on the idea that your company might be useful to them, your marketing defines you *and* your customer. A marketing process for your company becomes the foundation for your sales efforts and should be built first. Many startups and many businesses have no formal sales program—marketing alone generates sales. In more mature businesses, marketing lays the foundation for sales. Either way, marketing is a must.

From the perspective of your customer, there are stages that they must go through to get to a buying decision. This is often called the customer's *journey*. Usually in selling technical services to a complex business, what is up for sale is a solution specific to each customer's needs and problems. Closing this kind of business requires that the customer know and trust your company, understand what you do, and believe you can provide significant value or savings by solving their problem. That's a journey that requires you to deeply understand the problem, offer the perfect solution, and quote a good price. It's complicated—you're not selling cupcakes at a community bake sale!

If your sales staff is just relying on their experience or charm, and not following a plan for meeting with a fully prepared lead, you will get a mixed bag of customers. Some you can serve, but others you can't; some are profitable, while others aren't; some believe in you, and others don't click. Your customers, sales reps, and other employees will feel the imbalance and discord, and some will likely even defect to another company in your industry.

With a defined process, your sales team is in lockstep to bring prospects through a pipeline, to understand from data where each prospect is on that journey, and to be laser-focused on bringing the best—ideal—customers to a closed sale.

Sales and its processes are covered in great depth in upcoming chapters because nothing is more critical to the survival of a business than selling to customers. In the startup year, most expert founders spend time understanding their ideal customer and how to find them, and from this develop a clearer understanding of the customer's most satisfying journey.

Selling has a long learning curve. It's a skill that's often difficult for scientists. I was pretty introverted when I started my first business, and I had to learn that I was the ambassador of the business and had to connect with clients.

It's relational, not just transactional. You have the knowledge. Listen to your client, detect their pain points, and solve those problems with enthusiasm, confidence, and perseverance. As long as what you offer has value, success will follow. But in a team, everyone has to focus on the same value and communicate the same way if you want to build your business on serving the right customers!

Dr. Shane Needham

Founder, Alturas Analytics

DELIVERING TO CUSTOMERS

What does delivery to customers look like in your business? Are you doing physical work that generates material that must be shipped? Do you test material and generate results or reports? Do you sit in meetings with your customer and offer brilliant insights? Do you source or manage suppliers for clients?

No matter what you deliver, I urge you to think—from the beginning—about how your delivery looks from the customer's point of view.

What is most important to your customer? Speed? Quality? Format—can the customer port these data directly into their informatics system? Look even deeper. If your customer typically receives a result within ten days, do they evaluate you on how consistently you hit that average, or do they note only the few results that were delivered late? Do the aesthetics of your reports vary according to which staff member writes it, or do you teach everyone to conform to the same template and format?

At my last company's laboratory we learned, by listening to our best customers, that something as basic as shipping material is important. In response to customer feedback, we developed our shipping process to give the customer the impression that all of our work was of the highest quality:

- We learned it is critical that containers be clearly labeled, so to eliminate smudging, we used fast-drying ink in dedicated label printers and, once labels were applied, we taped over them with clear film.
- We discovered that some of our competitors shipped liquids in bottles that occasionally leaked or broke during air transit due to pressure changes inside airplane cargo holds. We solved this by using airtight sealed containers.
- We found out that shipping on Fridays sometimes results in shipments sitting in non-climate-controlled storage for

part of the weekend. We changed our shipping procedures and reminded our customers to do the same if they shipped material to us.

- We learned that international shipments require standardized documentation, but in some cases are still held randomly and without notice at borders. We engaged shipping brokers, marking all packages with directions to notify the broker in the event of a customs hold. The broker would immediately take action to clear the hold. Even though this carried a cost, our customers often gladly paid it, and if not, we did.

- We standardized boxes, vials, secondary containers, inserts, packing materials, and labels to project consistency and quality in packaging. The consistency of the packaging creates the impression of consistency in our work.

The contrast of some competitors' shipping processes was dramatic. From other companies, our customers might receive a reused Amazon box half-full of Styrofoam peanuts with a chemical sample semicontained in a glass bottle rattling around alongside a folded piece of paper with handwritten data. The attention to detail in our process communicated (subliminally) an impression of commitment to quality.

Every process and procedure, every label and report template, every delivery to your customer should follow a standard set of steps you've developed to address your understanding of the customer's needs. Human beings have a great capacity to remember what went wrong and to forget what goes right. Your objective is to minimize problems, and delivery is where you have greater control. The project or service itself may go awry at times, and your customer, while perhaps frustrated, will generally understand life's glitches and gremlins. But if you send reports that look different every time, or ship FedEx one time and UPS the next, you have only yourself to blame for the customer's impression that your operation lacks conformity.

Use the startup year to identify yourself and your company with flawless and careful order delivery and fulfillment. This is part of your brand. It may seem trivial to think of your shipping process as important—the dollar cost of shipping services is probably very small compared with what you charge for your services and expertise. However, these seemingly minor factors are visible parts of your business that set a tone about the overall quality of your operation.

GETTING PAID

Most accounting software can generate invoices, and if you don't have software, there are standard forms and templates online you can download. If you intend to steadily track your income and expenses, and manage your cash flow as I've recommended, I suggest subscribing to a cloud-based accounting software for time-saving and organizational advantages. For software with multiple price tiers, be sure to buy the level that includes a feature for sending invoices. If you don't want to do this yourself, hire a support person. For years, my company employed a part-time office manager for this purpose.

Here are a few things to keep in mind as you set up your back-office procedures.

First, send invoices as soon as you can. Your customers will pay you in a fixed amount of time—generally! Usually their accounting systems pay bills as late as possible, based on the agreed terms. If they agree to pay you within thirty days ("net 30" terms), they will receive your invoice, enter it in their system, and cut you a check thirty days after it was entered. Given the delays in mail service and bank holds on deposits, you might not have access to the funds until forty-five days after the invoice is generated.

Big companies tend to treat small ones very badly. Payment terms are often forced on vendors (that's you) with the understanding that the bigger dog gets to set the rules. Payment terms of ninety or even 120 days are no longer considered unusual, even though these same big companies effusively and publicly declare how much they value small enterprises for their talent concentration and innovative approaches. The fact is, these payment terms sometimes strangle small businesses, to the undeniable detriment of the larger R&D ecosystem. Unfortunately, you might not see a dollar from that fat contract for up to four and a half months.

If you've internalized anything I've written about cash flow during startup, apply it here toward managing cash flow at any stage of operations. Try pushing back on payment terms, as everything is negotiable. Whatever the terms, you must *always* send invoices out as soon as the work is complete according to your contract.

Unless it's a nonnegotiable customer requirement, do not make invoicing dependent on your customer's acceptance of your material or your report. When appropriate, require deposits to cover your commitments and materials costs. Don't supply an itemized list to the customer—simply ask for 30 percent or 50 percent (or whatever you feel you can reasonably get) up front, prior to initiation of the work. Your first responsibility is to your company and employees, so don't be afraid to enter into a negotiation over payment terms with a customer. Your job is to get paid as quickly as possible!

Request that customers pay you by bank transfer. Prepare a one-page form with your bank account and routing information and send it to new customers ahead of the first invoice. Include a standard US tax form, called Form W-9. Their accounts payable office will set your company up as a vendor in their system. For foreign transactions, this will be a wire transfer, and their bank will deduct a fee. If you include a standard wire transfer fee on your invoice, most customers will pay it.

If you ship materials to customers, include a standard shipping charge for each shipment. You are not Amazon Prime. Make the shipping charge sufficient to cover the actual ship charge, packing materials, and time your employee spends packaging and preparing paperwork for the shipment.

Finally, be diligent about monitoring your customers' payments. If a payment does not arrive within fifteen days of the due date (less if you're expecting an electronic transfer), send a reminder email. If you don't get a response, call their accounts payable office. If you are getting a runaround and the invoice is thirty days past due, mark the invoice as such and resend with a 1.5 percent interest charge. That often prompts payment— although the check may omit the interest!

A POCKET GUIDE TO THE STARTUP YEAR

In the startup year, you'll strive to make your company run more smoothly and efficiently, meaning more profitably. Operations will likely be the first of the three key functions you will work to optimize, making sure your team knows with each project what to do and how to do it. Operations has an impact on customer relationships, as executing all aspects of your business with consistency and conformity builds confidence in your ability to deliver.

Sales and marketing—the commercial function—will typically take longer to make efficient and process-driven. In the first year, concentrate on how you deliver proposals, invoices, reports, and packages to customers. Learn what works and what doesn't, and stay within your niche and target markets to avoid taking on nonideal customers.

Administratively, focus first on cash management: bookkeeping, payroll, billing, payment terms, and vendor relationships. Many owners learn to manage cash in their first business, so if that describes you, get schooled as much as you can in the first year or two.

You are laying the foundation to turn your company's offering—your deep and rich expertise—into a business that operates independently of you to deliver that expertise. Your goal is to build a business with value, and moving forward into the next section of this book, you'll learn to use the Four Value Signals (team, sales process, financial strength, and owner) as guideposts. In the first year, you will gradually but purposefully work *on* your business instead of *in* your business, transforming from expert to entrepreneur.

KEY TAKEAWAYS FROM CHAPTER 7

- The three basic functions of a business—operations, sales and marketing, and finance and administration—ultimately require independent leadership. At startup, all of these functions usually rest primarily on the owner's shoulders.
- Because you need to generate revenue right away, operations—delivering to your customer—is your primary focus during the first year. You're an expert, so use that expertise to create an efficient and consistent process.
- Every other aspect of your business runs more efficiently if you conform to a process-focused approach. In financial

terms, look first at managing cash flow. Build other administrative processes as needs develop.

- In sales, initially you're selling your expertise. Solutions for sale! Find out which customers benefit most, and you're on your way to developing a consistent sales process that brings you the best customers.

KEY TAKEAWAYS FROM SECTION ONE

- This is not a manual, but an orientation to starting a company. Founders often need peers, advisers, successful business leaders, and other specialized books or programs to fully flesh out their ideas and de-risk their plans. Don't be shy—asking "dumb" questions was my single best asset in starting my first company.
- Even if you plan to start a company that could become a commercial success—the next Uber or Genentech, for example—you will not likely start with millions of dollars and investors who will help catch you if you fail. To get to the point of commanding big resources, you have to first go through the startup phase.
- The path to successfully starting a company is emotional. You'll feel excited and discouraged, successful and self-deprecating, strong and terrified, visionary and uncertain. It's all part of the ride. Seek the advice of others, particularly those who have succeeded in similar ventures. Many will be generous in sharing their knowledge, helping you deal with those completely normal feelings.

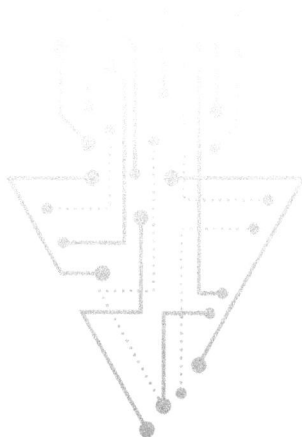

GROWING

"*The purpose of a business is to create a customer.*"

—PETER DRUCKER

"*The essence of strategy is choosing what not to do.*"

—MICHAEL PORTER

CHAPTER 8

THE BUSINESS CYCLE

In the beginning there is you: your idea, your plan, your energy, your money, your hard work, your worries and fears, your guts to go after the next sale. You may hire a worker—maybe a young person who doesn't cost much, or perhaps a contract worker or two. You'll probably see some initial success. After all, you've been talking up this idea and have some loyal friends who will throw a little work your way. You might get enough early business that you think, *Hey, this is pretty successful! I guess I am really as good as I thought.* You're in the honeymoon period.

Business slumps a bit, as your early customers who jumped to give you work have their needs met for now, thanks to your efforts. Revenue slows down. You worry about upcoming expenses and the new hire who doesn't have enough work to stay busy.

Business author Seth Godin wrote a book titled *The Dip: A Little Book That Teaches You When to Quit (and When to Stick).* The dip he describes acknowledges that this slowdown is part of the natural cycle of a business.

Business consultant Ichak Adizes, in his book *Corporate Lifecycles: How and Why Corporations Grow and Die and What to Do about It*, studied this initial period, placing it at the point where a business transitions from the exciting, energizing learning phase to pass through the dip to true growth. To get past the dip and into the growth cycle, you must make a plan to find, get, and keep customers...again and again. You learn quickly that it's not enough to put up a website and then wait for customers to magically find you. You learn that "If you build it, they will come" is magical thinking. You learn the most important thing a business does is get a customer.

If you figure this out and act, you pass Godin's dip, and your revenue goes up again, ideally higher and higher. Now, as you enjoy success, your competitors move to copy you and attempt to lure your customers with lower pricing. Your customers perhaps see your product or service as routine and look for the next bright, shiny object. Your revenues flatten and then fall.

Every business goes through this cycle, from a first flush of excitement, down into a dip, up a growth incline, and down again into a decline. This curve is shaped like an S laid on its side, and its mathematical name is "sigmoid curve."

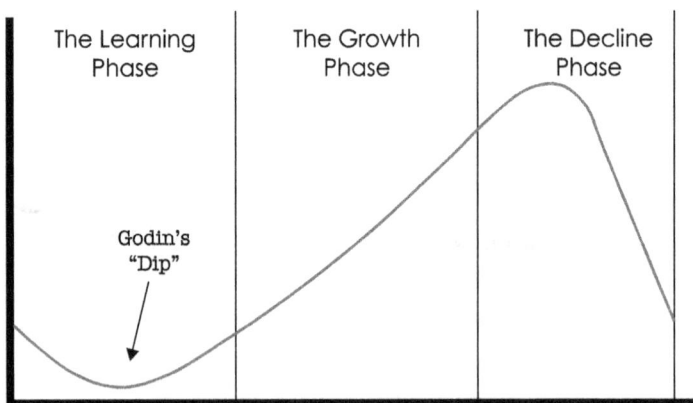

The Learning Phase | The Growth Phase | The Decline Phase

Godin's "Dip"

The sigmoid curve of business means that no matter your offering, your company and your market will be predictably challenged. You must go through a learning phase, move through the dip, and figure out how to sway customers to see your exciting valuable offer. Then, if you're wise and attentive, in anticipation of the coming decline, you fine-tune, reinvent, or extend your offer.

In essence, the business you're in now will not be forever. You must constantly think, *With these predictable challenges, how do I plan to grow?*

In life sciences outsource services businesses, the business sector in which I operated, a pattern has emerged over the last forty to fifty years. During this time, biopharmaceutical companies have ceased doing every single task of product development in-house. These are the steps in the cycle:

- A procedure within the pharma company becomes routine, and the company seeks outsource providers so it can save critical resources for more demanding tasks by handing over the routine one.
- The providers improve speed and automation for the routine task, because their goal of increasing profit margins drives them to do so.
- Competitors emerge, offering cost savings. In the past three decades, offshore providers have become very competitive due to reduced labor costs.
- The original outsourcing providers lose contracts. Their commoditization of the service, coupled with the emergence of lower-cost competitors, shuts them out of the market they developed.
- The original providers sometimes reinvent their offerings by bundling higher-value ancillary services together with the now low-margin commodity service.

As an example, think of the chemical compounds that must be tested for many properties before they can be considered likely candidates for drug development. One of these properties is solubility—if the drug doesn't dissolve in the gut, it can't pass into the bloodstream. This is a routine and boring measurement, so pharma companies trended toward outsourcing the work. Outsource providers specialized, automated, and worked to capture exclusive contracts from big pharmaceutical developers such as Pfizer and Merck.

Then offshore firms competed these away from early providers, who responded by developing more complex and specific assays with options to generate more information. Ancillary services—such as measurement of dissolution rate of the compounds, or improved sensitivity and precision of the measurement—offered higher value by making buying decisions contingent on more reliable data. The new and improved services helped advance the scientific approach to drug development, provided new value, and recaptured customers and profits for the outsource providers.

The universal business cycle—dip, growth, plateau, and decline—is inevitable. The ability of some providers to revitalize a declining business segment is a function of leadership. Leadership involves many skills, and as discussed, it's not all about being the best expert in your company. Effective leaders look forward into the future to anticipate change and plan for it. Effective leaders know about cycles. They constantly monitor their hard-won market share and measure their value to customers.

Growth in the face of the business cycle is possible for companies that are well-structured, in touch with their markets, and regularly measuring performance.

KEY TAKEAWAYS FROM CHAPTER 8

- All businesses have a common cycle. You can know what stage you're in and react properly if you're aware of the cycle's predictable ups and downs.
- The cycle has its origins in your success. The more successful you are, the more your competitors want your market share. The more customers you reach, the sooner they think of your offering as routine.
- An effective business leader analyzes during both low and high points of the cycle. If you get buried in daily business operations and fail to analyze, you will not see change in market trends coming around the bend. Experts look at their industriousness in the workplace setting. Entrepreneurs have an eye on the business and its future.

CHAPTER 9

CUSTOMERS

THE GOOD, THE BAD, AND THE UGLY

A customer—at the simplest level—is someone willing to pay for what you offer. If you make a nice pillow for one hundred dollars, I'll bet Mom would buy one. If your pillow inflates automatically to a preset fluffiness when a head hits it, early adopters who love new tech will buy it. But remember the universal business cycle: the honeymoon period, when a new business launches, is exciting and energizing, but then there's the dip. If you rely on Mom or the early adopters, you'll be in the dip as soon as their short-term need is met.

A sustainable, growing business is built on customers who receive significant value from your product that exceeds justification of the cost. These are people for whom your offering is a perfect fit, a solution to a problem they *must* fix. These customers are thrilled when you solve their problem because it removes a limitation on their company growth, they have a new way forward, and their future looks different and brighter. They love your solution. They return to you next time they have a problem, and ask for another solution. They praise your name to others who have a similar problem. In fact, they love to talk about their own success with alleviating this big headache, and how they solved it by choosing to work with you.

These customers are infinitely more valuable than Mom, despite her unconditional love and willingness to help. They represent repeat business and can give referrals, and once you have some ideal customers, finding more gets easier. The question to ask yourself when faced with a selection of prospects is this: *If I have to spend about the same amount of time and effort to bring on any new customer, why should I waste any effort on one that is difficult or not a good fit? Why don't I just focus on finding the good ones?*

See how easy business decisions can be?

We're talking about customers at the outset of this section because many business owners start out viewing a customer as anyone who will pay them anything to do anything. This might be expedient but not very efficient when starting up. A customer who wants a tiny project can require as much work and attentiveness as one with a big project—you still need to quote, onboard, initiate the project, position resources, deliver and report, and ship and receive materials. A customer who complains, micromanages, or otherwise demands too much attention costs much more in time and effort than one who trusts you and your team. Part of growing your business is realizing that and optimizing efficiency by finding and retaining your *best* customers.

This level of operational efficiency relies on your sales process. Remember, a defined, consistent, and successful *sales process* is one of the Four Value Signals I identify as indicators of the maturity and accrued value of the company you're building.

Let's assume you've been operating your company for a

couple of years and have worked with a variety of customers. Do any spring to mind that you should never have worked with?

Take a look at your customer list over the past year or two, if you've been operating that long. An old rule of thumb applies: 20 percent of your clientele demands 80 percent of your attention. Your best customers are the 20 percent who make up 80 percent of your revenue. The 80:20 rule almost always describes companies that have not narrowed their customer list.

Here is a truth worth internalizing. No matter how many social posts or advertisements you publish, how many hands you shake at conferences, how many mailing lists you buy, *you will never find all of your potential ideal customers.* You can afford to be picky.

If you have a random mix of good and bad customers in your book of business, bring your team together and do this:

- List customers by name, and label them *good* or *bad*. You can use the word *ugly*, too, to represent customers you don't yet have a good relationship with—and you're not sure where it's going.
- For each customer, guess at the weekly (or monthly) number of man-hours you spend. Re-sort the list based on any high-demand customers who are low return. If not expected to change, such customers might belong on the *bad* list.
- Estimate how much time you could free up for higher-value work if you were to eliminate some or all of the *bad* customers.
- If you can free up time to acquire or better serve ideal customers, resolve to release all of your worst customers as their current contracts end.

> Our biggest challenge in terms of customers was concentration. Our best customers liked us a lot and kept giving us business. We knew the dangers of having too much revenue coming from a few, but we had trouble refusing the business. This eventually came back to haunt us: in a single year, due to their own issues that were out of our control, we lost our top three clients and suffered a 35 percent drop in revenue. This threatened the survival of the business.
>
> Dr. Michael Kouchakdjian
>
> Founder, Blue Stream Laboratories

IDEAL CUSTOMERS

Ideal customers have a mix of features, but you will know them when you work with them.

First, ideal customers get more value out of working with you than others do because your solution is a perfect fit for their problem. Note that their perceived problem and what they say they need might differ. I define the customer's problem as the issue that's holding them back, costing them time and money, and maybe even impacting several of their goals. Imagine you sell laboratory supplies, and someone calls to say, "I need some cleaning fluid." The problem might be a dirty countertop (solving this is low value) or a need to validate sterility to a regulatory agency (solving this is very high value). It's your responsibility to figure out whether the customer stands to gain a little or a lot from your help.

Also, the ideal customer shares your way of looking at the world, aligns with your beliefs and principles. They get you, and you get them. Not about religion or politics—although in some businesses, these might be important avenues for connecting providers with customers. Think instead about the business you founded based on your belief that you offer amazing benefits—then match yourself with a customer who believes that too.

Imagine an amazing coffee shop that has multiple approaches to brewing—drip, cold brew, espresso, pour-over, percolated—and knows how to match each one with the right roast and coffee varietal to create the perfect cup for each customer. My wife maintains she can't taste the differences between various coffees and brewing methods, and she opts for whatever Starbucks variety is featured for the day. I believe, with all my soul, that I can have a great coffee experience by getting the right combination of coffee and brewing. So as a customer, I'm a better fit for the fancy coffee shop, no question. (By the way, I recommend Intelligentsia's downtown Chicago cafés.)

My last company established a reputation for clever, results-driven experimentation to develop methods for customers. Other companies in the same sector are known for flawlessly carrying out standardized and accepted procedures with no experimentation. The belief of the customer—about which is the best way to conduct scientific investigation—is fundamental to their choice of a lab services provider.

Think back to the discussion in Chapter 2 about values. Can you reframe some of your personal values to better align with your core beliefs about what your business brings to others? Many times, entrepreneurs choose company values that reflect their personal beliefs but do not connect them with their ideal customers. For example, if your business is in a sector known for high-quality work—precision machine parts that always fit and last for years, for example—then *quality* is a strong value of yours, but it is not necessarily one that helps connect with a customer in a world where every such maker also values quality. Many of your personal values might not quite express what makes your company different. If you choose a word like *reliability* and tell your customer about the lifetime and wear-resistance of your parts so they have a lower total cost of ownership, you might be closer to communicating what you really mean by *quality*.

Last, your ideal customer fits a profile you can identify. Even among scientists—let's say in the biopharma world, where I worked—differences in mindset and approach are vast and reflected in many cases by externally identifiable traits. Venture-backed companies or bootstrappers? Boomers or Gen X professionals? Suburban office complex or hip urban space? Overworked and worn down, or vital and fit? Young or old, academic or corporate, conforming in appearance or iconoclastic? Starbucks or Intelligentsia?

The customer's profile is important not because it determines how valuable your solution might be, but because it helps you position yourself in the customer's world. What images or attributes in your marketing will catch the eye of your target customer? What issues concern them? What do they find exciting or fun?

All of that might sound silly or irrelevant at first—in a highly technical field, with technical customers, all that counts are objectively assessed capabilities, right? Nope. Customers are human, and they want to believe you can relate to them. If you do, then of course you're going to understand their problems. If what you project resonates with them, you will be more successful in connecting with them.

You probably don't want to get *so* specific in defining your target customer's persona or avatar that, for example, you only do business with fans of the Boston Red Sox and never work for New York Yankees fans. But there is a world's difference between talking with a startup founder who is a professor at Stanford and an exec who just landed a $60 million venture capital investment in San Francisco.

Today, the companies I work with spend a lot of time and

thought defining their ideal client profile. Doing so involves digging into records and experiences from the sales team to the bench scientists, and surveying both good and bad past customers about their experiences and opinions. Well-understood attributes of the best customers help guide marketing, define a sales process, and build out the best team to deliver efficiently.

A lot of people talk about pivoting these days. I felt we needed to remain focused on our target customers and deliver what we knew how to do really well. People always want to go after new ideas, and there's a danger in pursuing everything that seems like a good opportunity. We defined our services tightly—our niche is really well defined. That makes it easy to just ask someone, "Do you need this?"

We weren't pricing low like a big provider might—our model was quality, not price. Maybe this cut us out of trying to get the big companies as customers. It seems like they always want providers to compete on price. Our customers returned to us a lot, and we didn't hear them talk about price.

Also, in that ecosystem of smaller companies we work with, people move around every few years. So over time we got known pretty widely in the industry. By staying focused on what we did well, we ultimately didn't have to do a lot of marketing. It felt like a lot of our sales came to us.

Dr. Robert Suto

Founder and CEO, Xtal BioStructures

Identify your ideal customer's profile, belief system, and potential problems. Describe your ideal customer in detail—you want to know one when you first meet them so you'll position your business more clearly in prospects' minds, and your ideal customers will quickly find you.

CLARITY

I can imagine that at this point you might be thinking, *Hold on. If I limit myself to only my ideal customers, I'll miss working with other people who might need my help. I can't reject someone who wants to pay me!* I won't insist that you refuse to work with anyone, but let's consider a couple of important points.

First, what are the consequences of working with a customer for whom you're not a perfect fit? Either they don't get maximum value from you, or you're forced to tailor what you usually offer to their somewhat different needs. Someone comes to you and asks, "Can you help us with this problem?" It's a bit outside your wheelhouse, but you think, *Well, we* can *do some related things. Maybe if we did what they need we could expand our offerings. And if we're successful, this will be a good way to build our reputation.*

That may be tempting, but there are some potential traps. One is that you stand a greater chance of coming up short. Either you don't fully deliver so the customer must finish solving the problem elsewhere, or the customer is unhappy with the quality of your work. You probably also put in extra time and effort trying to fix the situation, and in the end the project isn't profitable. You're not going to get repeat business.

Maybe you take on this project because you were already thinking of offering this service, so the job gives you a chance to get some experience. Perhaps you've been working on a plan to launch this new offering. You were going to invest in new equipment, get some training and testing under your belt, and position the new offer on value.

But if these things were not done and you just dive in, what was all the planning for? If you planned to be more successful, why give up the success? And if you have no plan, why aren't you acting as a leader?

Sometimes taking a risk turns out OK. The bold player wins the contest, right? I don't want to discourage you, but I caution you to do one thing before trying to help this new customer: *tell them that what they are asking for is not currently within your core capabilities.* Offer to recommend someone if they prefer, but if you do try it, let them know they must accept some risk. By doing this, you maintain and strengthen your credibility with existing customers—and this new one. The trust that comes from credibility pays off.

I once talked with a prospect who wanted my lab to develop a method to purify ten kilograms of a drug. This amount was beyond the scale we could handle, so I described our capabilities and told them we weren't a good fit. I recommended a competitor—a rival—and thanked them for thinking of us. I also called the rival company and told them to expect the call.

Four weeks later the prospect called me back. "The other guys said they couldn't find a method to do it. Can you help in any way?" We ended up developing the needed method and formally transferring it to my competitor, for which we made more than $40,000. Because I developed credibility with honesty and a referral, and because I also used the opportunity to clarify my core offerings, I changed my nonideal customer to an ideal one. I left them with a positive impression of my company that made them want to work with me. They looked more critically at their problems until they found something I could help with. And they came back to us with more projects over the next few years!

Staying within your specific niche is important for you and all your customers. But clarity is the most important reason tightly and narrowly defining your niche. Remember the "narrow is better" concept from Chapter 5? It works here too—defining what you offer narrowly helps you stay narrowly focused on the customer who will gain the most from working with you. For the benefit of you, your staff, and your customer, *find a way to express with crystalline clarity what you do.* Use words that express it in terms of the value your ideal customer will receive from working with you.

If you don't communicate to your ideal customer with pinpoint clarity, a competitor will. And sometimes that's all it takes for your competitor to lure your ideal customer away from you.

KEY TAKEAWAYS FROM CHAPTER 9

- An ideal customer receives maximum value from working with you. They believe, just like you, that what you offer is important and solves problems. They will repeat, and they will refer.
- Taking time to identify ideal customers, instead of taking on all comers, pays huge dividends in time savings, increased profitability, and satisfaction—for you, your employees, and your customers.
- Once you know who your ideal customers are, you can be *much* clearer and more effective in the way you market and sell to them. That clarity will not only help you connect with the right customers, but it can also convert a customer outside your target market into one you can work with.

CHAPTER 10

MARKETING

With a clear understanding of why you need to build your business to find and serve your ideal or best customers, you might ask, "OK, so how do I find these ideal customers and convince them my company is the best fit for them?" It all starts with marketing—with customers' needs in mind.

I am abundantly aware that as trained analytical thinkers, scientists and engineers are skeptical of marketing. We see it as shiny packaging meant to hide flaws, a subterfuge, possibly even lies meant to trick us into looking at a product. We tend to perceive marketing as being about the product and the seller, not about us as customers. The first thing we might typically ask of a salesperson is, "Cut out the marketing and tell me how this works." We probably don't consider that the only reason we're in a sales conversation is because, through marketing, the company conveyed to us that there might be something valuable here. But if a company's marketing is built on trying to connect with us, as buyers with needs and problems, it helps us understand that the company is likely to be credible, trustworthy, and maybe even helpful.

This is a starting point to understanding that customers

must *become* ready to buy: *marketing brings us prospects we can then sell to.* With this understanding—that people must go through stages to become customers—you will be able to help guide them on their journey. You will be much better poised to identify your ideal customers and develop a sales process, and your revenue growth will be determined by how well you define and connect with your market, not by how many hours you stay in the office.

It is fair to say that the line between marketing and selling is fuzzy. Today's marketing happens largely in the digital domain, where behavior is trackable. You can bring a customer closer to the point of interest without much personal attention, using a lot of automated tools. Good marketing saves a lot of time and effort in selling. But especially with a complex project or a technical sale, you can't get a customer all the way to placing an order without working closely with them to define the project. There is a point where marketing ends and selling begins.

In the process of acquiring a customer, marketing functions to make your company visible. Marketing helps prospects understand what you do, and can cause prospects to wonder if doing business with you could benefit them. That's a journey—they need to discover who you are, what you do, and why they might want to take action. Everyone is busy. Nearly 100 percent of our brain's bandwidth is consumed with our own lives, jobs, and conversations. We do not willingly or randomly choose to admit new information, and if it intrudes on us, we give it only fleeting attention and thought. It's unreasonable to expect potential customers to do all the work of finding us, understanding us, and figuring out how we might help.

As a frequent conference speaker, I often talk about marketing as the foundation for a sales process. A sales conversation can happen only when a potential customer, a prospect, starts to think about whether there's any value in engaging with you. The sales conversation is your opportunity to clarify what you do, connect that directly to the prospect's problems, and determine whether your solution can solve their problem. Only then can you pitch yourself as the best solution, or craft a custom approach that fixes their problem. Such a discussion can be very quick if your service is simple (sharpening kitchen knives, for example), slower if you need to specify the scope of work (cleaning an office suite), or even slower if you must craft a custom proposal for a complex sale (developing engineering specifications to construct a building).

When you are a young company, usually your services are limited, less complex, and easy to describe. Marketing designed to bring your prospect to the point of considering the value and benefit of working with you might then bring them to a point where they are nearly ready to buy. Many small companies do not have a sales force. Instead, the founder or a senior team member makes direct contact with prospects to qualify and complete the sale. Using your marketing program to do the lion's share of your sales work is a great way to save money as your company starts to grow, but this strategy relies on tight targeting. You must design your program to connect with ideal customers, avoiding broad targets, and your message and positioning must be very clear. As addressed in the last chapter, the more clearly you understand your ideal customer's needs, beliefs, and traits, the easier it is to connect and communicate clearly.

Without marketing, your sales activity—whether it's just you or a sales team—will have varying, unpredictable rates of success. Your sales team will be more successful if your company makes the effort to connect with potential ideal customers, instead of connecting with *every* potential customer. You will attract and retain better and more talented salespeople. If your marketing is not properly designed and functioning, any good sales representative you hire will likely quit, frustrated by the lack of support from their employer who lacks a marketing strategy.

Well-executed marketing plans have multiple functions: establishing and communicating a corporate and personal brand, establishing authority, improving consistency of messaging, automating customer acquisitions, and—through modern analytics—tracking market changes. The formerly distinct field of public relations (PR) has in many aspects merged with traditional marketing through social media applications. PR used to send messaging widely to print media outlets, but these outlets have narrowed to reporting only large business deals. Now, social media, blogs, and online resources have much greater reach. Modern marketing leverages the digital domain in myriad ways.

Although marketing is foundational to selling, it also operates in parallel with the sales process. In the past, selling was all about the sales representative establishing a relationship with the customer, and salespeople were taught clever techniques to manipulate that relationship to close deals. To those salespeople, marketing only served to make their brands noticed and established. Now, when customers spend more time online investigating your positioning in the marketplace than they do talking with you, marketing must be multifaceted and serve several purposes.

In a successful approach to marketing, your message, the positioning of your company, the value statements about your offerings—whatever aspect your marketing efforts are developing—must be concise and used in all aspects of company communications. Spending on marketing is wasted if it paints you in an unclear way. A blurry image makes it more difficult for your prospects to understand who you are, what you do, and why they will benefit from your help. A good program and good leadership ensure that every aspect of company communications is on message. Through clarity and repetition, customers hear the message the way you intend it to be heard. This goes beyond your website, social posts, and ads. Every employee should communicate the same messages about your company, whether to a delivery person, a neighbor during a backyard barbecue, or a colleague at a conference. You never know where your next customer is coming from.

Marketing is tough for scientists. I had two years' experience in marketing before founding my first company, and that helped. At the outset I was the face of my company, but given the importance of social marketing these days, I knew I needed help. I hired a marcom [marketing communications] person and that has been quite successful.

To establish credibility, I turned to my team. We pulled together presentations for conferences and wrote articles for trade journals. We did a good job of presenting ourselves as thought leaders with valuable technical capabilities. Our marketing communications built on these, and we were successful in picking up new clients.

It takes time and work to make your communications authentic, effective, and impactful. You need to speak with reporters, respond to comments online, and create thought content that teaches and informs.

Some prospects learn about me through word of mouth, but then they vet me online. The content on the site—the number of articles and the value of the content, and my personal and company brand credibility—leads people to contact me. That's the goal, but it took time to build up that presence and make the content communicate our reputation and values! Marketing properly is a marathon, not a sprint.

Dr. Judy Carmody

Founder, Avatar Pharmaceutical Services and Carmody Quality Solutions

PERSONAL AND CORPORATE BRANDING

As you now know, the primary function of marketing is to take your ideal customer on a journey from being completely unaware of your company and its valuable solution…to knowing who you are and something about what you do…to making a personal connection with you…to realizing your offering might be useful to them. These steps might be thought of as activation barriers, but at each juncture you have to put a little energy into the relationship to help it along. At each step the customer must decide to accompany you to the next, and they don't have to. If I already have a new smartphone, I might not even notice the iPhone 47 has been released.

Branding efforts make your company visible and identifiable with its offers. Company name, logo, and tagline are not designed to communicate in depth with the customer but to provide a shorthand recognition mechanism of the real entity with a real offer. Think of the flag on the uniform of an Olympic athlete—it doesn't function as a statement or a decoration but as an identifier.

CORPORATE BRANDING

Corporate branding is not so complicated when thought of in simple terms. You want your company name to be memorable and connected with what you do for two reasons: (1) you want a potential customer to be able to find you when they begin to wonder if you might be of use to them, and (2) you want a satisfied customer to remember you when they run into someone else with a similar problem. If prospective customers can remember your company name and product, they can likely find your website, email, and phone number.

Big companies spend a lot on their corporate brands. They

dominate in their markets because their customers identify them with their products. Big corporations want their logos to be distinctive, their taglines to be memorable, and their style to be consistent. Often, though, a smaller company emphasizes a more personal brand—think of the hippie feel to Ben & Jerry's ice cream packaging, or the fact that landscaping companies almost always have green in their logos. The name, logo, colors, and shapes are all chosen with an emphasis on their resonance with the company brand. That resonance is desirable because the human mind is built of gazillions of memory connections, which amplify one another when they connect back to a concept.

PERSONAL BRANDING

So, what makes personal branding distinct from corporate branding? Remember our discussion about the persona or avatar for your ideal customer? Your personal branding helps your ideal customer understand your persona. In the beginning, when your company is very small, you as owner are a big part of that persona. You set the tone for the company culture, you hire people who are good fits in personality, and you connect with customers based partly on the company persona that emerges.

One of your objectives is to define your company's personal brand around values and mission, uniqueness of approach and philosophy, and how you work with customers and deliver success. As discussed previously, you'll sell to people who believe what you believe, so occasionally revisit your mission and values to make sure they align with your ideal customer's perception of your value.

Big corporations get less leverage from presenting a personal brand, because the idea that one hundred thousand employees might share a persona seems disingenuous. But that doesn't mean they don't try. A personal aspect, liked shared values, can help a company's message resonate more strongly with a customer, and this tends to be a more powerful approach to facilitating connection when your company is smaller. Big corporations get more muscle from their position as market leaders, because the consumer loves the safety of buying what the masses buy.

Sometimes personal brand seems to catch on across an industry, and then it just gets silly. For a time in the early 2000s in Boston's biotech world, CEOs and venture capitalists took to wearing ragged jeans and Hawaiian shirts. This faux-hacker aesthetic, borrowed from Silicon Valley, was thought to communicate a personality that cared less about dress code and more about getting things done. Instead of "We're from Wall Street," it was fashioned to convey "We're in the trenches, working all hours, and having fun!" When everyone started doing it, they just looked like sheep (and poseurs).

In making any choice about personal brand, stay authentic and true to yourself, and consider what will connect with your customer and set you apart in a positive way. Some of your brand attributes will align you with your industry, some with your values, and some with your ideal customer. Appearance, visible work ethic and process, your website, and all of your integrated collateral materials are part of your personal branding.

Do not spend a lot of forced effort and money on developing a personal brand. Among scientists, this doesn't count so much as communicating to a customer your values and expertise. However, if some part of your corporate personality or culture emerges, and it's within accepted standards of professionalism in your field, run with it! You might find it helps you outshine competitors.

THE STORY AND THE HERO

The best branding hints at what you really bring to your customer: not a thing or a capability, but a way to get past or through their problem. Marketing specialist Donald Miller, in his excellent book *Building a StoryBrand: Clarify Your Message So Customers Will Listen*, equates successful branding with telling a story and notes that there is a formula for good storytelling. It is seen in the best movies and books, and it breaks down simply.

The main character needs to get somewhere, achieve something, become something, and has a problem that stands in the way. A guide shows up and offers teaching, a roadmap, a method. The guide is experienced whereas the main character is not, but can't solve the problem *for* the character. Instead, with the guide's help and through increasing strength and self-belief, the character makes a transition and becomes someone new, finds love and acceptance, overcomes adversity, wins the game, and gains status, wealth, and self-esteem. In short, this is the hero of the story.

Miller points out that you can incorporate this formula, which resonates with all human beings, into your marketing if you do this: make your customer the hero, and you be the guide.

That's right—you are not the hero in the story. Instead, you possess what the hero needs—even if they don't know it yet—to achieve their needed growth transition and become a winner. If the customer is the hero, you're the sage who is guiding them from weak to strong.

There's no need for me to elaborate much about how to do this, because you can always read *Building a StoryBrand* yourself. The book is built on a firm foundation of work: philosopher Joseph Campbell's classic *The Hero's Journey* introduced this arc to many of us, including George Lucas, who used it to plot the

Star Wars movies. Obi-Wan Kenobi and Yoda are the guides who help Luke Skywalker become the hero.

To earn his trust, Obi-Wan and Yoda had only to show Luke three things: their credibility (they could do what they said they could), authority (their willingness to demonstrate and teach), and understanding of Luke's need.

CREDIBILITY, AUTHORITY, AND UNDERSTANDING

Credibility comes from personal brand, behavior, and track record. You are credible only if you're trusted, and we talk about that a little more in the next chapter. Your track record is what you used to start your company. Your deep expertise in your field and knowing how to apply it bring value to your customer.

Your customer will accept you as a guide if you were once a hero. And you were—you developed the path, method, and experience in the course of becoming an expert. You succeeded or won when you figured out how to turn your expertise into a business. You learned, became an authority, and now you are a founder, leader, and hero.

Leverage your authority and status. Demonstrate what you do best and teach it to others. Take the best stuff you know, and show your customers how to do it themselves. "Uh…wait," you say. "Won't that undermine the basic purpose of my business, which is to *sell* what we know, not *give* it away?"

The answer is no, and I have a great example that proves it.

In the early 2000s, Marcus Sheridan and some partners founded River Pools and Spas in Virginia. The company sold in-ground fiberglass pools, not custom cement ones and not above-ground pool kits. It was a good enough product that by 2007, the company was doing about $4 million per year in revenue and spending $250,000 on marketing. When the great recession hit in 2009, orders evaporated as consumer spending dropped off a cliff. But in 2011, the company did $7.5 million in revenue on a marketing spend of only $20,000. River Pools is now one of the top ten pool companies in the United States—and it still sells only in-ground fiberglass pools.

The *New York Times* interviewed Sheridan in 2013 about his secret to success in a slumped market. It was simple. He decided to try blogging about what he knew. His first, and most famous, blog post is titled, "How Much Is My Fiberglass Pool Really Going to Cost?" Now, if you're thinking of getting a pool, and you're responsibly googling to find out about costs, what are you likely to type in the search bar?

Sheridan's next blog post was an honest discussion of the drawbacks to fiberglass pools as compared with concrete. One of his next blogs listed some concrete pool competitors that all made high-quality pools. No one else in the industry talked honestly about the competitors, the product's pluses and minuses, and the costs. River Pools today posts a lot of great video blogs, but it still doesn't do expensive print advertising. And the fiberglass pool orders keep pouring in.

This story illustrates the power of authority to build trust, connect with your exact ideal customers, and establish yourself as a guide. Is there a downside? Can you give away too much? I don't think so. After learning that you are an authority, your busy (probably overworked) customer is *not* going to say, "Great! Now I know how to do what those guys can do. I'm just going to carve out another hour in my day and do that, too!"

Start small with authority marketing, and watch it work. Put together a page-length PDF file titled "Five things you should know about…[insert major problem in your customer's industry]." Provide people a link to download it in as many ways as you can—social media, business cards, notes on conference bulletin boards, your mailing list, postcards, whatever. Create a landing page for the article on your company website, and require a name and an email address in exchange for the free download. If it touches a real problem your customers share, you will get names of leads. And, by the way, your customers will not actually do what's on your one-pager. They will only scan it. If they want to do what it says, they know their best approach is to talk to you.

MARKETING IN THE DIGITAL WORLD

These days, most of us understand that everything we do in the digital domain—social media, web search, interaction with individual sites—is trackable, and is likely tracked. We may not understand how the information gathered about our behavior is used, but we accept that it is being used in some way. There are clearly problems with this system, but there are some benefits to analysis of user behavior.

Let's assume you're using analytical data from various tools to track user interaction with your website and social media sites. Here are a few possible beneficial advantages to doing that:

- Improving your site's navigational flow so visitors can easily find what they need
- Learning what content is most engaging for visitors so you can produce more of that
- Learning what fails to engage so you can make those features better or eliminate them
- Finding out more about your ideal customers' interests so you can develop your business around what's most important to them

- Better clarifying your message by paying attention to your visitors' behavior

To best serve your customers, you need to know their response to what you offer and how you present it. The best way to do this used to be by asking them, perhaps using survey cards in the mail or follow-up phone calls. Now, you can look directly at their behavior: how long they hover to read something, which links they click, where you are getting the greatest engagement geographically, and so on. This helps you understand who is drawn to your site and why.

I consulted for a French-Canadian company that had not been analyzing its website traffic. Quebec law requires sites to be presented in both French and English. By analyzing traffic to each part of their site, we learned that the French site was primarily visited by job seekers, while the English version engaged visitors looking at the company's core services. Much more was to be learned from the data, but even this simplest of analyses—where the visitors clicked first—told us much about user engagement patterns.

Another consulting client had a site that had not been updated in nearly twenty years. The content reflected what the company offered, but an analysis of user behavior showed that the way the website's content was presented—as a single PDF file, instead of within a navigable page structure that could guide the viewer's journey—was out of step with what visitors were used to navigating. Because visitors to the site couldn't immediately figure out where to go to get what they needed, very few moved beyond the first page. More than 80 percent of visitors searched for the company's name rather than a product or service they offered. Analysis of user behavior showed that visitors searched for the company name, clicked to the site, and then hovered at the company phone number. This company's website was no more effective than a listing in the yellow pages.

You will be coached by your website developer to install analytics. The next step, too often ignored, is to study your site's traffic and visitor behavior. If your business is very small, trends will emerge over time. If you have many visitors, perhaps because you sell something through your website, you can try things like testing engagement levels with different messages. Website analytics can monitor not only where someone clicks, but how long they hover over a text box or hold-click on a pull-down menu.

If you collect email addresses from sales leads, you'll learn even more. Once a visitor joins your email list, your site automatically tracks their visits by name, and you can learn how the behavior of your most engaged visitors (those who have given you their address) differs from those who find you through a search engine.

You can learn a lot about your customers by analyzing the way they engage with your website's content, your emailed messages, or your social posts. Visitors that go after the high-value content, clicking and downloading and hovering to read, are more likely to be your ideal customers. Until you prove your ability to engage those customers, you probably won't gain anything by spending a lot of money on things like a more professional logo design.

MESSAGE

One of my first nonscientific talks was to a trade group of lab services companies, much like my own. I spoke about the value of a consistent message, noting that both the consistency and the message are important.

Consistency means that anytime anyone hears about your company, they hear the same message. Remember that your customers take a journey toward doing business with you. You want them to make a personal connection, to think about how you might fit into their plans, to ascertain whether your offering could be useful or helpful to them. That's the ideal time for you to bring a potential customer into the sales part of your conversation. Psychologically, this is a longer journey than one might assume. Remember the last time you formed a personal connection with a product: *Gee, maybe it's time I took a look at updating my smartphone. Those new features look pretty cool.* That might feel like an instantaneous revelation—you don't hold vivid memories of all the product exposure or its marketing that got you to that point. You only realize the point when the conscious mind takes control.

An air-conditioning service business in my smallish town has five employees and three trucks. One truck is new and has a great decal with the logo on the side. Two of the trucks are old—one has an older logo design the company no longer uses, and the other has no signage at all. The employees wear their own clothes to work, and based on appearance there's no way to tell they work for this company—not even a cap with a logo. When asked about what they do, maybe one says, "I repair air conditioners," and another says, "My company installs commercial HVAC systems," and yet another says, "We handle heating and cooling needs across the tri-county area."

This inconsistency reduces the opportunity to move any potential customer to making a personal connection with this business. It might mean another company with consistent messaging, let's say a company from the bigger city forty miles north, can make inroads with local customers here if it expands its reach. Being the only game in town for some time, the local company has become complacent in its messaging.

Statistics say your message must touch a potential future customer as many as eighteen to twenty-four times before they start to make a personal connection, so you can understand why a big corporation might spend millions on its graphic identity, print advertising, Internet ads, and even television commercials. As a small company working in a narrow niche, you probably can't do this. But you *can* strive for consistency in messaging, making sure your logo and tagline are always visible, and that your offer and value to the customer are described concisely and with the same phrasing every time. Most of all, realize that your employees, vendors, contractors, and support servicers all touch other people, so if they talk about your company, you want them to relay the same messaging.

Employees won't instinctively do this, so you have to teach them. This is the *message* part of "consistent message." There are countless books on messaging, and I've conducted workshops for clients on developing and implementing messaging strategy. Proper messaging is formulaic: What's the customer's problem or need? Who are you as a company? What does a successful solution look like?

"Ever lose heating in the winter, or AC in the summer? Miserable, right? Our company, Bob's Heating and Cooling, makes sure all the homes in the tri-county area are comfortable year-round." If you teach that phrase, it's not going to stick instantly—not in your mind, nor in the minds of your employees.

I know a business owner who carries an unfolded wallet with crisp five-dollar bills in his jacket pocket. Occasionally, he says to a random employee, "Tell me what we do." If the employee can come back with the company message, they get a new five-dollar bill. It takes time, but employees learn to do it, and in the process, they learn that consistent messaging is important to you and to the company. For full disclosure, I read about this exact trick in business books by two different authors, so it doesn't belong to me or my friend. Try it—and remember, crisp new unfolded bills!

A SALES AND MARKETING FUNNEL

I've been talking about marketing as if it were passive. You have a logo, a website, and a brand identity that showcase your authority and a consistent message so customers will come to you when they're ready to enter the sales process. *Oh, how we all wish it would work that way.*

Sometimes they *will* come to you. The phone will ring, or someone will fill in the contact form on your website. This is called "inbound marketing" by those who want to help you establish and promote your brand and optimize your digital domain presence. Inbound marketing works—if you've made yourself easier to find over your competitors—for a customer who is urgently trying to solve a specific problem you have claimed you can solve.

If you want *more* customers, you must reach out. Remember that many customers frame their problems only in terms of an easily described need, and their expression of need does not necessarily reflect the impact of solving the problem. In my field of analytical chemistry services for drug development, a customer might express a need as such: "We need someone who can do this assay."

"OK, we can," I might say. "But hey, can you tell me a little more about what you're trying to achieve?" Listening to the answer and asking more about their goals, I might hear that they are trying to build a business case for moving a new drug into clinical trials. Beyond "this assay," what else can my company offer to help?

An inbound customer has often decided what they want, and

it may be difficult to shift them away from their fixation on the thing they think they need from you. After all, they contacted you about exactly what you advertised—of course they want you to give them what they asked for, instead of your asking a bunch of questions. But if you reach out to customers at the right moment, instead of letting their current need connect them to you, you have more opportunity to talk about how you might help with this and other needs.

Imagine you have a list of prospects—say, two hundred to two thousand names if you're a smallish company—that you've initially qualified as possible ideal customers. You collected their cards at a targeted trade show, or maybe you bought a database of "companies developing cancer drugs."

Better yet, develop a lead magnet.

A lead magnet is simply an invitation offering something with value. "Get a free list of five key _____ that will help you _____." "Click here to watch and learn a three-minute trick to _____." "Join my FREE webinar to learn how to _____." You can put an opt-in button in a social post, an online ad, or a QR code in a poster at a conference.

Lead magnets are mostly delivered online these days, but the process is the same as when you mailed in an ad from a magazine to get a free "how to" guide. The process is transactional; you give up your email in exchange for something that has a bit of value to you. Sure, it means you're going to hear from the company every now and again by email, but you can always unsubscribe. An interested person—one who gives their email to get the lead magnet—is by nature prequalified. They want to learn what you know. They've decided they might get something useful from you.

Don't waste the time of those on your growing email list by sending newsletters or continually asking for a phone call. These people are a little interested in something you offer. Nurture their interest by continuing to extend even more value—if you don't, they will unsubscribe. The great thing about a list of email addresses from people who opted into receiving your content is that you have their permission to increase their awareness and understanding to the point that they may make a personal connection. When they make that connection, they probably already know more about how you might help than someone who asks, "Can you do this assay?"

This email list you're nurturing is called a marketing funnel. Once you are sending your marketing funnel regular tidbits of valuable content, you should occasionally—say, every fourth email or so—ask them to do something. This is the beginning of inviting them into a sales conversation. Those who are ready will take action. Donald Miller, author of *Building a StoryBrand*, which encourages you to be the guide to your customer hero, points out that the guide must not only give the growing hero the tools and knowledge to achieve their goal, but also tell them to act. Obi-Wan Kenobi does not say to Luke, "Hey, maybe you could try a little of the Force?" You must call your potential customer to action, because if they actually have a problem, they will then identify with the solution you offer.

- "For our loyal subscribers only: 20 percent off this valuable course until the end of the month!"
- "Click here to get your coupon for a free cinnamon bun on your next visit."
- "For a limited time, we are offering a free one-year service contract to those who buy one of our control systems."
- "Receive a free consultation and diagnostic visit from a senior team leader if you act now. Find out if upgrading your current system will save you money."

These are all calls to action that may be attractive to a prospect who's been following your authority marketing. A click on a call to action is an invitation to talk. That's the transition from marketing to selling!

A RECOMMENDATION

Arguably, by far the best and most comprehensive book on marketing and PR in the new (predominantly digital) world is online marketing strategist David Meerman Scott's *The New Rules of Marketing and PR: How to Use Social Media, Online Video, Mobile Applications, Blogs, News Releases, and Viral Marketing to Reach Buyers Directly*. Scott makes such a tremendous effort to stay current and relevant in our rapidly changing world that his book, in its eighth edition as of this writing, is updated with a completely revised new edition every two to three years. The book is loaded with ideas, and I highly recommend it for a deep dive into online marketing tactics.

KEY TAKEAWAYS FROM CHAPTER 10

- Marketing and sales are related but have separate functions. They represent two sequential programs that, through your stepwise and consistent action, bring a potential ideal customer on a journey to becoming a buyer of your product or service.
- Marketing has many functions and technologies, but at its heart it is the foundation of your sales activity. Savvy marketing helps you locate your ideal customer by aligning your brand and message with their beliefs and needs. Marketing readies a customer to have a conversation about how you might help them solve a problem.

- Marketing in the digital domain—social media, online media, emailing, analytics—offers many tools a small company can use to be successful without spending a fortune in time or money. Many of these tools use automation to nurture a prospect into a ready-to-buy state, taking a lot of work off the hands of an overworked team and ensuring consistency in your company's message and process.

CHAPTER 11

SELLING

Having established a brand, developed credibility using your authority, and set up an automated flow of nurturing emails to stay in the minds of customers and occasionally call them to action, you have mastered the basics of marketing. Selling is the next logical step—helping the customer complete the rest of their journey toward agreeing to buy.

If yours is a young, small business with an offer that is fairly easy to understand, your marketing program may be sufficient to bring prospects in a near ready-to-buy state. The action of selling to someone who contacts you about a specific product or service is often straightforward. Finish qualifying (are they close enough to your ideal customer profile?), find out about the problem they need to solve so you know whether your solution is complete or on target, discuss pricing, and ask when they are ready to get started. You probably don't need a sales team at this point—you or one of your top technical experts, with a little training and experience, can often complete the sale. It doesn't have to be anyone's full-time job.

I'm going to continue to refer to the match between the customer's problem and your solution as the reason why sales happen.

It is true that sometimes people buy for reasons that don't look like problems—an unexpected windfall of cash is a great reason to buy a luxury car. But that luxury car buyer still wants something they don't have—status, prestige, a balm for a midlife crisis, to get the best of a rival…or maybe their dream since childhood has been to own a Porsche. Buying that car solves one of those problems, and the best car salesperson wants to know which it is.

If what you sell is more complex—for example, it requires a detailed understanding of the customer's internal structure and their problem to configure the best solution—marketing alone will not substitute for engaging deeply with the customer to complete a sale. The process of getting to a deal is longer and requires more skill in this case. You must probe with a lot of questions, strive to understand all the customer's alternatives to solving the problems, and negotiate on delivery process and price—and *both of you* will develop a deep understanding of the value your solution offers. You'll probably write a detailed proposal for circulation and negotiation before signing the deal. But at the end you'll probably be able to close the deal simply by asking if they're ready to get started.

You may hate selling. Many technically or scientifically trained people hate selling because they feel—quite honestly— that their value comes from being the best. You may hire a salesperson to avoid having to do sales, and then be dissatisfied because your salesperson does not share your enthusiasm about the benefits of your offer. A favorite aphorism of sales guru Brian Tracy, author of *The Psychology of Selling*, was that all selling really is a transfer of enthusiasm.

It is *your* job, not the customer's, to determine whether they are a good fit for your company's offering. You must first understand the depth and breadth of the customer's problem, and the value of applying your solution. You'll be enthusiastic if you are certain that—for the customer—it's worth taking on, spending money, and acting now. You've found a customer you can help, so go ahead—transfer your enthusiasm!

THIS IS WHAT SELLING IS:

- Asking lots of questions
- Finding out where your solution will have an impact, positive or negative
- Understanding if the customer's statement of "need" accurately reflects their problem
- Recognizing the time impact on all the customer's processes of solving or not solving the problem
- Calculating cost of alternative solutions, especially those the customer uses now
- Checking what you're learning against the customer's perception
- Discussing alternatives—even competitive ones—with the customer
- Keeping the discussion focused on the problem so the right solution emerges
- Presenting your solution, but only once you know its value
- Referring the customer or recommending another solution if yours is not the best fit

THIS IS WHAT SELLING IS *NOT*:

- Assuming that what the customer asked for is all they need
- Giving a PowerPoint presentation of your capabilities before knowing which ones might be valuable
- Talking in detail about price without first understanding value

- Presenting a smorgasbord of options and hoping the customer will pick the best one
- Offering your solution before the customer engages in a discussion with you about their problem
- Canned scripts or practiced taglines that manipulate the customer with sleight-of-hand or psychological techniques

THE WRONG WAY TO SELL

Selling is about establishing a productive relationship with a customer. You and the customer are both human, and I'm sure you've had *some* experience with human relationships. Dating offers a great comparison to sales: you want to establish a rapport with the person you're interested in, and to do that you want them to see you as trustworthy, credible, and likeable. To sell something, you might not need to achieve the same standard of likeability, but credibility and trust are certainly part of the sales game. To build those, you need to be granted permission to have a conversation, establish common experience and interest, and not jump too fast to "Do you want to go to dinner?"

Think of the most recent connection request you accepted on a social media channel. It *seemed* like a valuable connection—until within minutes your new best friend has sent a description of a great offer and a request to schedule a call. I get up to ten of these weekly, and it's clear many don't even know what I do. Why would I engage in a discussion of someone's offer before I've established that I have a problem they might solve? How do they even know if I am the type of person, or have the type of business, their offer might help?

If you try to sell to someone who doesn't need or benefit from your offering, you're wasting your time and theirs. If you try to date someone who's not interested, ditto.

Even if your company is a fit—you can fulfill the customer's need and offer a benefit—you fail to sell correctly by not appreciating the customer's process. If you move faster than they can or are willing to, you're ignoring their need to understand your benefit on their terms. Even an ideal customer may not be ready at the point you start to engage. Perhaps other problems or jobs are more pressing, or another solution already solves their problem. The customer must first wonder if there's a need, and then connect "different" or "better" to you and your company. They can now respond to your invitation, because their problem is important enough to start thinking about a solution.

A sales process that doesn't allow the customer to take the necessary journey is like asking someone to marry you on the first date. If you're worried about a misstep, just remember that there are only two wrong ways to sell: The first is to try to sell to the wrong customer. The second is to use a sales process that doesn't recognize the customer's journey.

If you feel that by selling you are somehow violating your principles and your objectivity, that you might misrepresent your scientific integrity—stop that. People who feel this way are almost unable to push, lie to, or cheat a customer. On the contrary, you'll probably bend over backward to make sure your customer knows all their alternatives. Although you might make missteps along the way, if you keep the customer's needs in mind, that's never wrong.

THE SALES/MARKETING BRIDGE

How do you go about inviting the right customer at the right time to a sales conversation? That's what marketing is for. If the information in your blogs, videos, ads, interviews, nurture emails, podcasts, and website content is designed to engage the right people, you can assume that those who regularly see it are beginning to make a personal connection to your offer and your expertise. You need to invite them to interact directly with you—if they are ready.

A call to action, or CTA, is your request that the customer make the decision to engage. Plan to add some CTA to every fourth or fifth nurturing contact. *Schedule a Call* and *Find Out More* are examples of CTAs. Note that those should offer something, such as a partial solution to a problem addressed in your nurturing email. Any of the following can be effective if someone is interested in content to be released later: *Get on the Wait List. Subscribe Now. Sign Up for the Webinar.* This one is good too: *Interested in knowing more? Download our handy guide.*

A potential ideal customer who is early in their journey with you may not be at the level of recognizing a need. In many cases they will ignore you and may not even notice the presence of a CTA in the material they read. A direct CTA asks a prospect to talk or buy—that's a bigger ask than an indirect CTA such as *Download Our White Paper*. Still, a low-cost purchase converts a prospect to a customer by a small commitment, making it easier for them to engage in a conversation about other services you might offer. The most important thing you can do is recognize that, in bridging from marketing to talking to ultimately selling to customers, you must extend an invitation. The customer then gets to make a choice to engage with you in the next step.

A customer response to an indirect CTA, like *Sign Up for Our Webinar*, lets you know they are interested in learning if you could be useful to them, and some number of them will gradually recognize your credibility and develop trust. With that trust in place, you can insert a more direct CTA in a future message that lets them make the choice to engage more deeply. When a prospect takes some action in response to your request, it's OK to directly reach out with a thank-you and an offer to help: *I saw you downloaded our white paper on thermal bath calibration. Just wanted to reach out to see if there's anything else about our baths or their regulation that I can send you. What are you working with now?* That's an invitation to engage in a conversation about doing business.

I think of the steps a customer takes—from becoming aware of you to buying—as a staircase. Each step requires a little commitment and energy on their part. Your job is to offer a hand and invite them up to the next step. Marketing helps them understand, gradually, what you offer, encouraging them to make a personal connection as to how your company might be useful to them. The step into a sales conversation is a response to your invitation to talk, and you guided them to this point by first building trust. They just have to take a little step up to say yes.

As a business owner, you can help, guide, and invite, but you cannot push. Pushing—for example, buying a conversation with an invitation to an expensive lunch—creates the illusion of movement up the staircase but without really gaining a fully engaged customer. Buy meals and send gifts, and you'll get meetings but perhaps little in return in terms of sales.

Leverage your marketing technology and automated nurturing process to offer an occasional CTA, and start conversations with those who opt in. Or reach out by cold-calling, emailing, and directly messaging to ask to engage with individual prospects: *I notice you've read some of our blog posts on _____. I want to reach out to thank you, and I have some additional material I can send you about _____. When is a good time to schedule a call so I can learn about your needs and share what I have that can help?* With an acceptance, the prospect crosses the bridge from marketing to sales.

This conversation is the first point at which you are allowed to discuss their need, and with a growing understanding of their need, to talk about their problem. Remember that their perceived need is sometimes an incomplete expression of the true problem—a partial picture, or even a consequence of the problem rather than its root cause. Often the real problem has impacts beyond those ones that are most pressing for the person you're speaking with. For example, after a discussion about the customer's issues, you might say something like, "Sounds like your legacy software is not only a training burden for the research team, but it's a huge headache for the IT department who must archive the data. Have I got that right?"

With an opportunity to understand the customer's current situation, how they got there, and where they really want to be, you can begin to understand how to craft a solution. This is often called a *discovery process* in sales lingo. I think of it as gauging the gap between where they are now and where they need to be, and more important, then analyzing that gap and expanding it. By expanding the gap I mean helping the customer see that the problem and its impacts reach beyond their own need. A question like "Who else is impacted if this doesn't get done on time?" often makes a customer think beyond the way their own situation is affected by the problem, and it increases the value of your solution.

Once you have an idea for a solution, present it to the customer and talk through how it will help, how it will be delivered and supported, and what they will gain from it. If there are any concerns or objections to what you propose, address those accordingly or adjust your proposal. You can then ask, "Do you want to go ahead with this?"

This last question is called *closing* a sale. The question sounds nonthreatening, doesn't it? That's your objective—to make closing nonthreatening to the customer, framing it as an invitation and not a task, and to avoid the fear reaction some salespeople have around closing a sale.

Every step up the staircase is an invitation, not a push. This way of thinking about the sales process eliminates the classic view of sales as pushy or manipulative. It is a successful approach because the focus is on the customer's problem, placing control in the customer's hands and thereby establishing trust. Trust is of paramount importance. If, in your gap analysis, you determine there is not enough gain for the customer by paying for your solution, you must say so. Delivering on the promised solution and value, and continuing to support your customer, strengthen that trust bond and turn the customer into a long-term fan. Fans buy again, and they recommend and refer you to other ideal customers.

This way of thinking about selling—putting the customer and their issue at the center, rather than upstaging with your business needs and capabilities—takes a lot of pressure off scientists in a selling situation. We're trained to be objective, skeptical, and analytical. If we push a sale, we're none of those things—we've put our solution first and will accept anyone who buys it. We've used none of our core skills in problem evaluation and solution. If we think of selling as something that leverages our core scientific skills, and not as a ploy meant to deceive or obfuscate just to get a mercenary win, we remove the mental block to selling well.

If you accept that as a scientist you are equipped to be a strong salesperson, all I have left to do is orient you to the four main steps of a sales process: (1) *Qualifying* is understanding whether or not you and the prospect are a fit for each other. (2) *Gap analysis* is identifying and quantifying the problem and its impact. (3) *Presenting* is showcasing your solution—how it solves the problem and how valuable its result will be. (4) *Closing* is bringing the deal together and getting a commitment to start a project or purchase order.

As we've gotten much bigger, I can't be involved in every sales situation. I try to spend most of my time with our most valuable prospects and clients. I feel like a therapist whose job is to listen to their problems, but I feel really comfortable in that environment. Nothing makes me happier than figuring out if I can solve a problem.

It's still selling. In sales, you respond to emotion in the situation, and I like the immediacy of that. I'm less comfortable with marketing because I get bored—I can't see an immediate return, and I need constant feedback from people. There's nothing better than the good feedback that comes from having done something that's quantifiably useful.

Laura Browne

CEO, Covalent Bonds

QUALIFYING YOUR PROSPECT

You offer a solution to *some* customers' problems. Your value is in matching your solution to their problem. In a rational world—in which the customer and you both fully understand all aspects of the problem and the solution, and act upon that understanding—that value translates directly to price. It's a very objective alignment, which will appeal to scientists! In winning a customer, you have to make this deal as rational as you can.

How closely does the prospect match your ideal customer profile? If the match is poor, the prospect is less likely to see your value, so you're not a good fit for each other. Fit issues can come from misalignment of values or beliefs—they can be personal—but more often it's a question of whether your services can really solve their problem, or whether their urgency is great enough. The benefit the customer receives must be significantly—and quantifiably—larger than the cost.

Go back to your analysis, from a few chapters ago, of your good and bad customers. In most cases, the good ones were those who got a big return on their investment, while the bad ones didn't. Even if the conflict seemed more personal with the bad customers, if you look closely, you may find their dislike was rooted in dissatisfaction with the value they felt they were getting.

If the fit looks good, you'll more quickly develop rapport with the prospect, and growing trust allows you to discover the rest of what you need to know to qualify them. Do they have money, do they need to solve the problem now, and how will they make a decision?

BANISH THE BANT METHOD

An old set of criteria for qualifying a prospect, still used in a lot of sales programs, uses the acronym BANT: budget, authority (to make a decision), need, and timeline. This is old-fashioned and frequently guides salespeople to ask the wrong questions.

Remember, your customer does not recognize their problem and, therefore, does not have the tools to evaluate the situation or a possible solution.

Yet, what the customer usually recognizes is a *need*:

- A need is a new car, but the problem might be service record, expanding family, new job, or desire for increased status.
- A need is to test a drug for hypertension, but the problem might be a stinging failure (in front of management) in a past approach, inherent instability in the chosen lead compounds, poor exposure of the drug as dosed, or the desire to make one last try before eliminating a poorly performing program.
- A need is a new website, but the problem might be poor messaging, aging images or content, changes in user engagement, lack of a seamlessly integrated sales platform, or mediocre application of marketing analytics.

Customers mentally latch onto a perceived need as a shortcut to solving the problem. Think of how your own mind works. If something is driving you crazy, you probably think of the issue itself, not the underlying causes of the issue. Once you sit down to consider all aspects of the problem—causes, impacts, costs—you probably don't get far before your mind jumps to problem-solving. And, if you had time to solve the problem you would have done it a long time ago.

Before looking at better alternative approaches, let's consider the drawbacks of using BANT, assuming the above description of the customer's thought process is accurate:

Budget. Why is budget (the amount the customer planned to spend on this need) important if the problem hasn't been thoroughly investigated? If the problem is costly enough, the budget is not important—only the savings of the solution.

Authority. If it is a problem only for a low-level employee and not the whole organization, you don't necessarily need to search for the decision makers. None of them care. If it is a broad-stroke issue, and you can establish and clarify that, anyone in the organization will be interested in a solution. You will be able to engage those who have the authority to spend on solving it. Decision-making no longer rests with one leader—CEO, VP, or director.

Need. Again, not the same as the problem. The expressed need is a starting point for your investigation. The person you're meeting with will express only their own need, whereas the problem may impact more than just that person's business unit—and the breadth of such impact drives the buying decision.

Timeline. What you really want to know is, "Do you need to solve this now, or can it wait?" Without recognizing the problem, your prospect can't know the answer. Your investigation instead uncovers the urgency behind their issues. If it's not urgent, the value in your solution is likely low at this time.

WHAT TO DO INSTEAD

Selling is a conversation between a solution provider (you) and a potential customer with a problem. That conversation is about whether you understand the problem and its impacts and can match your solution to that problem. If you've been using BANT or something similar to qualify, adjust your thinking.

Don't ask about *budget*, but immediately start establishing client credibility. Research the customer and possible sources of their need, and make sure they're likely to have funds. If they don't have the money, that's not the same as not having allocated budget! If they don't have funds, you may get a future win by recommending a more affordable approach for now.

Forget individual *authority*, and ask how they will evaluate whether to go ahead. Dig into details here, especially if you suspect you'll be helping others in the organization beyond your initial contact. You're looking for people who have high influence in the departments impacted by the problem. Many people in a functional organization have enough influence to contribute to a decision, and team decision-making is the norm. Once you identify the impacts of solving the problem, the individual authority of the person who contacted you is unimportant. Your ability to discover all the impacted leaders or groups helps you understand who might be involved in the decision to buy.

Don't equate *need* and problem. My favorite question when a customer mentions what they need is: "Why is that a problem?" I might ask this several times, and have to explain why, but my customers will finally get it: the need is born from the problem, and if we solve the problem the need goes away. Talk about *why* it's a problem now, *whom* the problem affects, *how* the client has tried to solve it, *what* specific impacts have resulted, and *how much* time cost has been lost from not solving the problem.

Finally, *timelines* are not defined unless the urgency is ascertained. A highly expensive problem is often more urgent, but not always! Sometimes the problem can be identified and quantified, but other priorities are often more important and should be addressed first to clear a path to implement your solution.

You will sometimes find you have a bigger role than your customer does in establishing the value of your solution. That's because they have not thought through the problem, impacts, or costs. You absolutely should have a greater role in uncovering the impacts of the unsolved problem as compared with the wonderful future when the solution is in place. In effect, you expand the value of your solution by fully evaluating the problem. This is not a trick to increase your price. It's a demonstration of your authority and your value to your customer. Once you've identified all aspects of their problem, including those they hadn't thought about, your customer will be glad they are working with you.

My last company specialized in purifying drug compounds that were extremely difficult to work with. We separated molecules from nearly identical isomers that were, in essence, mirror images of each other. The value of doing this work increased as the compounds grew in importance to our customer—as it became clear they were potentially viable drugs in clinical trials. We recognized quickly that to purify a gram of material to be used in some early tests had lower value than purifying a kilogram of material needed for advanced long-term trials. But helping our customers with the low-value, less urgent work at the early stages meant they would come to us when the stakes were higher. As our customers scaled up, we were intensely aware of the value equation!

GAP ANALYSIS

The difference between your customer's current state and their desired future state is called the *gap*. The gap is central to your success in a sales conversation. You must understand the gap, because it determines the value of your solution to the customer.

The gap belongs to the customer, not you. Imagine you sell minivans. Your customer's gap—the scope of the problem your minivan could solve—might be related to a growing family, a move to a new school system requiring carpooling, a business that requires hauling audiovisual equipment to a job site, a need to transport a family member who uses a wheelchair, a couple wanting to spend a summer car camping, or a dog walker with a pickup service. (By the way, all those possibilities came from me—a scientist, not a car salesman—riffing on minivan applications for a couple of minutes.)

Obviously, the features available in your minivan models will have different values to different users. Seating, storage, adaptability, customization, styling, electronic controls, sound system—your customer will evaluate every feature your minivans have or don't have against their own perceived need. Of course, their need is not necessarily the full scope of the problem. Need does not always represent all of the impacts your solution might have.

The car-camping couple says they want a van that doubles as a camper, but they may have removable seats and a nice sound system in mind. The video-and-sound business might be interested in storage and styling. And either customer might have kids and need to carpool occasionally. *Note to self: always ask minivan customers if they have kids!* It is your job, if you intend to sell that minivan, to uncover the value attached to every possible feature you can offer. Imagine taking your customer from their current expressed need ("We want room for six kids and we don't have enough space") to their ideal future state ("Room for six kids, *and* a great safety record, easy to clean, comfy to drive, plus it's *quiet!*"). What is that worth?

By asking questions about the current and future state, you expand the customer's awareness of their whole situation. They're shopping because they think a minivan might be a good fit for their need—that's why they came to you to talk and look. As you explore the problems or needs this van could address, you confirm that the customer came to the right place. With every feature you discover that has value to them, you also expand their perception of the real value of the minivan. Assuming you can find, *and help the customer articulate*, the value of eight features instead of the one or two that brought them in to look, you expand the value of crossing the gap and they increase their planned spending.

If you have ever bought or sold something from a catalog, a price list, or an online site, you've experienced buying based on need alone. Buyers judge the product against only their need and budget because no one expands or analyzes the gap. In developing a product price list, sellers can't include the gap in the price calculation, except in a general sense—what is the value of this to the average customer? A price list implies to some buyers that you sell a commodity product, and they may look for comparable products (again based only on need) before buying.

You, the expert for whom this book was written, are selling your products and services based on your unique and valuable capability to deliver something only you can. Your expertise has many aspects and can be applied to solve various problems in different ways. A customer seeking your ability to solve a problem, and wanting the highest return on their investment, is not buying a commodity. To meet each unique customer challenge, you configure a quote to the specific problem.

Put in the effort to understand your customer's gap. You get greater returns from your sales efforts when you present a solution developed from a detailed understanding of the problem and the gap. The inclusion of some of these techniques allows you to give more to—and gain more from—your ideal customer.

The best recent book on selling to the gap is titled *Gap Selling: Getting the Customer to Yes* by Keenan. I recommend it to those who want to improve their sales skills. However, as with anything you want to learn deeply enough to groove the skill—to make it familiar and easy—you must practice. Get with a partner, sales trainer, or sales team, and make role-playing sessions part of your culture of ongoing development.

> We never talk about how great our products are until it is absolutely necessary. We want to be in a conversation with a customer about their challenges. We want to understand empathetically and provide the best solution. I've closed deals without ever showing a PowerPoint or a demo of our software. Those are just distractions from understanding their real needs and learning if we can even provide the best solution.
>
> Dr. Joseph Simpkins
>
> Founder, Virscidian Inc.

PRESENTING

In a classical description of a sales process, after you've defined the problem, you *present* the solution. Unfortunately, in our technology-obsessed culture, presenting seems to have become synonymous with PowerPoint slide decks. To a salesperson who doesn't know gap analysis, or understand how a need differs from a problem, that PowerPoint deck is a crutch. It's usually a series of self-serving slides about the company: its history, size, capabilities, product or service lines, and some testimonials to prove how great they are. Presenting that deck—often at the outset of the sales conversation—is how an inexperienced salesperson avoids the analysis and solution development. As scientists, we have a self-limiting belief that sales is not science, and we default to what we think a scientist should do: show slides.

Under the StoryBrand concept championed by Donald Miller, that kind of salesperson presents the company as the hero. But you know better! Your company is the guide. Your customer will be the hero, with your help. The guide helps the hero achieve success by offering a solution to the hero's problem. While finding the gap, analyzing and extending the gap, configuring the best solution, and pricing appropriately, you must keep everything centered on the problem.

Whether you offer your solution, once it is developed, in a slide presentation to a management team or in a written proposal, *offer it to the customer's problem.* State the problem first. Don't introduce yourself or your company—simply start with the problem and its impacts. Next, describe the product or service you know will solve the problem, then introduce the implementation plan. Finally, forecast the future state of the happy customer whose problem is solved. Use language and images to help them visualize the projected improvements. If you present verbally first and on paper later, follow the same format for both presentations.

Near the end of a proposal or slide deck, I like to include a page or slide that indicates my company was created and developed to solve precisely the type of problem the presentation was about. I stop short of talking about every service we provide, presenting only the capabilities we've used to develop the presented solution. I'm reminding them we serve as guides, by virtue of having been heroes ourselves in the past. But that's one slide, or one paragraph, and it's not what leads the proposal.

A verbal or slide proposal is great, but in our world of complex technical solutions, a proposal in electronic document form serves a couple of important functions.

- The proposal ensures all discussions across the customer organization focus on the same problem. Anyone asking, "Should we do this?" knows exactly why they should.
- The proposal points to the problem's multiple impacts. In case I missed some impacts in my gap analysis, the expan-

sion of the problem in my proposal helps my customer wonder in what other areas the solution might help.

- The small conversations that often take place during gap analysis can, over time, become confusing to the customer. We talked about many things, and some of those conversations might not have even been properly centered on the problem. A well-crafted proposal removes any confusion the customer might have in recalling how we got from our first meeting to a final cost.

With a proposal in front of all the important influencers and decision makers, it's time to guide the customer to one last step. On the sales staircase, every step takes a little customer energy, and the willingness to step up comes when they are prepared… and when they are invited. It's time to close the sale.

CLOSING

Closing used to be the skill at the heart of every sales program, the skill most valued among professional salespeople. Selling was often seen as a competitive sport: the salesperson against the customer. Winning was everything, and the most complex sales were closed by master tacticians. The glory of winning, just like in chess, was the close—the checkmate, the moment the customer caves and accepts the deal. Have you seen Alec Baldwin as the evil sales manager in the 1992 film *Glengarry Glen Ross*?

By teaching closing as the key move in a cutthroat game, the sales profession was not serving itself well. Closing moves or techniques played out like a shark strike, an unexpected checkmate, a sneak attack. Pros deployed closes to confuse or manipulate a customer. A summation statement sales trainers commonly used was, "And now the customer almost has to say yes." It smacks of manipulation. It sounds like your whole job is to back your customer into a corner, leaving them no way out. That's no way to treat your ideal customers.

Sales guru Brian Tracy offered a famous weekend workshop called "The Psychology of Selling" (and later a book of the same name). At the end of the workshop, he shot off a rapid-fire delivery listing dozens of closes, each with a name such as "The Ascending Close" or "The Sudden Death Close." Tracy gave salespeople who are afraid of closing—and fear is not unusual, given the high stakes in a big sale—some assurance that there are ways to prepare the playing field to their advantage. He taught that by not paying attention to the way customers make big decisions, salespeople can take risks. It's not *necessarily* true that these named closes are tricks or manipulations, although any could be applied that way by an unscrupulous salesperson who values the sale more than creating value for a customer.

Assuming I've done my job in keeping the focus on the problem while presenting my solution, I like to make two slight adjustments to my approach. These are not manipulative tricks but serve to focus the customer's thinking once again on the problem and its solution.

1. First, instead of asking the customer if they would like to get started, I often say, "*When* would you like to get started?" By presuming they are as ready as I am to start today, I not only show my preparedness, but I also trust they are ready to go, too. If we've gone over the problem, and they know it's costly and needs to be solved soon, this question encourages them to visualize starting the solution. Asking "Would you like to get started?" is less specific, and might refer only to signing the proposal.

2. After asking something inoffensive like, "When would you like to get started?" my second technique is to *stop talking*. Silence is a great tool that communicates confidence, shows respect for the customer's thinking process, and often makes people a little nervous, and they feel as if they have to fill that void.

Even though I find many closing tactics of the past to be manipulative, I have trained myself to ask for the deal in the most inspiring way as I invite someone to step up to the last stair to become my customer.

STRATEGIES TO END THE CONVERSATION

You should be aware of two strategic concerns surrounding the close. These are not strategies to win, but instead strategies to prepare yourself for the end of the sales conversation.

Step Up

Just like every other step up the sales ladder, you are inviting the customer to step up. Signing on a big deal—and *big* is relative, depending on the customer's experience and authority—is a big step. It might not come easily to your customer, no matter how well you have identified and quantified the gap.

A customer may stall or object to closing the deal for reasons that are not always clear. Last-minute objections to closing, based on cost or some other concern, are normal and inevitable. Often the customer is just trying to buy time because they are nervous about making a mistake or missing something. For your customer, a lot is riding on this deal: Did they do all their research? Get the best price? Miss an alternative they hadn't considered?

Recognize that psychologically this customer has a need to slow down and feel certain. Some people are reluctant to move too fast with any salesperson. Maybe they had a past buying experience in which they felt manipulated, and they don't want to repeat the mistake.

If you have properly analyzed the gap and worked with your customer, attached their cost to *not* solving the problem, established credibility by asking the right questions—and if your solution is significantly less costly than the continuing problem—you should have everything you need to calmly respond to an objection.

Be Ready to Actually Close

When a customer says yes to your offer to go ahead, you must be ready to go ahead. This seems like a no-brainer, but it is a frequent oversight! The conversation goes better than you thought, the customer's urgency is high, and their style is to make snap decisions. You find yourself closing a deal ahead of your plan. There is nothing wrong with this, but if you've got a draft proposal with you and it has a signature line, you stand a much greater chance of completing the transaction than if you have to go back to the office to prepare one.

If they sign that proposal, be prepared to sign it as well. Whatever your process for finalizing with a customer, be ready. Make on-screen edits to the proposal if you're on Zoom, pen and ink if you're in the customer's office. Use a secure document signature application to get it signed. Know your possible starting time frame so you can give the assurance needed. As the scout motto says, "Be Prepared!"

Closing is not a trick, nor is it a source of suspicion for the customer or a source of fear for you. It's simply the end of a conversation in which you, better than anyone else the customer has spoken with, made your best effort to understand what can really help.

KEY TAKEAWAYS FROM CHAPTER 11

- A well-designed marketing program helps you ensure that when you engage in a sales discussion it is with the right prospect—one that may become an ideal customer. A sales conversation asks the customer to come on a journey or climb a staircase. If you recognize the journey they have to make and which step they are on, you will sell effectively.
- Old-school sales approaches, such as qualifying on BANT and sales presentation capabilities, don't work well when the sale is a solution to a complex problem—the kind of product or service we typically offer as experts. Think of yourself as a professional investigator. Your role is similar to a physician moving from a patient's complaint to the diagnosis. You are a helping partner, working to understand the best way to increase efficiency and profitability of their business.
- If you can help your customer understand the gap between their current situation and the best future state, you will be able to craft a convincing proposal, profitably price the solution, handle any customer objections, and confidently close the sale.

CHAPTER 12

OPERATIONS

If the role of sales and marketing is to feed the machine, and that of finance and administration is to keep the machine oiled and fueled, then operations *is* the machine. *Operations* means the production and delivery of product and service.

In services companies—anything from laboratory analyses to carpet cleaning—production and delivery are built early so revenue starts coming in. If expensive equipment is needed to deliver the planned services, that equipment needs to be installed and tested before it can be used.

In product companies, sometimes additional investment is required before sales can happen. In companies that manufacture or supply, products are often accumulated in inventory before being shipped to customers to generate revenue. In product development businesses entering an R&D cycle to develop a product, prototyping or *proof of concept* is usually demonstrated by an initial investment. Later, production and delivery needs can start once R&D completes, either through building manufacturing capacity or by contract manufacturing.

The difference between the product and services models are often logistical, but in most cases it's fair to assume there will be some cost in readying to engage with and deliver to a customer. In both models, money has to be spent before money can be made, so there's always pressure to get that delivery going quickly.

Think about these three elements when building out operations:

- **Process.** How the delivery is optimized and repeated
- **Management.** How the people involved in production and delivery work best together
- **Customer service.** How the delivery and ongoing connection with the customer will be achieved and will facilitate future sales

You can begin to see how the business function of operations is so important to the success of sales and marketing, which in turn brings in orders that keep operations running and its staff employed. Operations involves not only production and delivery of services, but it must also be part of the general functioning of the business.

Sometimes it is hard to separate operations from administration. In many companies, for example, human resources is viewed as an administrative function. I'd argue that HR is better placed as a key component of operations. HR should be process-driven, functioning the same for everyone. And most of your hiring will be concerned with production and delivery.

More important, the interweave between the strength of sales and marketing and the strength of operations—the push and pull between meeting demand and having the capacity to produce—argues that by treating employees as your keys to success in business implies that having the right people and culture is central to that success. To treat HR as simply an administrative task of employment law compliance, taxes, and benefits is to trivialize its vital importance to how the company competes.

Operations is not the most important part of business—it doesn't supersede sales or finance. It may have the largest employee base and require the greatest management oversight, but without sales and marketing it will quickly die, and without finance and administration it will at best falter and sputter along. Remember, this is the machine we're talking about!

I was a consultant functioning as sort of a connector or a matchmaker—clients outsourced business connections to me. My pitch was that if you use me to connect you with the right partner, you'll get better results, and I will prove that.

But soon everyone was saying, "You know, seeing the better results is something we've never been able to do before. We can find our own connections, but seeing the results is new." I needed to build the company around the productivity analytics, which was a different operational challenge.

That's when I found my business partner, who is a genius at analytics. She holds me accountable as well, which has been really valuable. I'm still sales, but with her running operations it just organically came together—from the client feedback on what was valuable to finding a partner who really understood that. It was the clients who told us what we had to do, but the right people made it work.

One thing I like about being on my own is that I can find the right people, or build the right systems, to accomplish the things I don't like to do!

Laura Browne

CEO, Covalent Bonds

A PROCESS FOR EVERYTHING

Repetitive tasks, or collections of repetitive tasks, are best built out as processes. The very act of defining and creating a process requires thinking and modeling, and that forces looking for the most efficient way of doing things. Assembly lines and just-in-time inventory systems are famous examples of process thinking in manufacturing. Employees can be deployed optimally according to their training and skillsets. Operating procedures can be written, and checklists developed, to assure consistent quality in manufacturing products or delivering services. Training programs can be developed from these so new employees become productive more quickly.

For your business to be efficient, no matter how complex, it has to be executed as a series of repetitive tasks. Each project may require a different number or series or order of those tasks, but they are all repeatable. Think back to your training in your field: the things you learned were defined the same way for everyone. In the workplace, you further developed your expertise by choosing the right tasks, optimizing them and the way they fit together, and thereby making your employer more successful. Your team can do the same, with your help.

Perhaps the most important reason to establish processes is that deviations, slowdowns, choke points, and so on are more easily identified and corrected. To do this, start by measuring the efficiency of each process to see how it's performing and examine ways to improve the metric. The act of measuring, in and of itself, leads to improvement—employees who know their work is being measured or evaluated take more care and thought into their jobs. The act of thinking generates ideas for improvements, and internal competitiveness kicks in—*How can I get faster at this?*—enhancing productivity.

Building operational processes starts with listing the self-contained operations. Commonly, production and delivery come at the end of the sales process, so let's start there. A customer agrees to a quote or a proposal and payment terms, and all of this is entered into a tracking system, or at least written on a whiteboard. The sales function is finished, and it's time to kick operations into gear.

The beginning of delivering services to meet the needs of a project might include ordering supplies or materials from vendors, receipt of materials from the customer, scheduling and team briefing, and so on. You might decide these tasks fall under a superprocess called *onboarding*. Onboarding might solidify the plans to accomplish a project, deliver on an order, or add a new client. You can create operating procedures for any and all of these.

If your proposal includes a custom service plan, the resources, timelines, and communication strategy must be developed. The project is carried out using a combination of services, each of which can be defined and completed according to a standardized process. The delivery of services, or the material your services produce—for example, your company manufactures and delivers a shampoo to the customer's specification and formula—can and should also be done according to a standard procedure.

The product must be shipped, the service completed, the results of a project reported, quality checked in some way, the project or order closed, and an invoice sent—more standardizable procedures.

Consistently and efficiently completing work sends your customer a message that it's time to review the project. This phase can tie back into sales (checking in on future needs) and also move forward to customer service (monitoring customer satisfaction and offering product support). Efficiency and consistency also send a message about your quality and attention to detail. Many customers carry out periodic audits of, or at least make regular informal visits to, their suppliers and service providers, and quality is always evaluated. A common customer request is to examine your training records and standard operating procedures.

You can incorporate your message of efficiency and consistency into other aspects of your business, and you should. When your work, your employees, your marketing, or your customer service process touch your customer, make sure they include your message.

At my last company, we knew our competitors' shipments to customers often included packaging and paperwork that were inconsistent. By building a consistent shipping process with attention to detail, we communicated indirectly that our level of care and attention was higher. Proper documentation, safety data sheets, secondary containment of materials to prevent spills, consistent box sizes, and use of recyclable packing materials were all built into our process. We even produced a short video on how we handled incoming and outgoing shipments. We called it "The Life of Your Sample" and ran it on the first page of our website.

The video wasn't really about us, and the way we did the lab work wasn't unique, but the subliminal take-home message was in what else it showed: the sample processing only took about one quarter of the length of the video. The rest featured a technician unpacking, logging, coding, and storing the sample...then later packaging, labeling, and carefully filling a highly protective shipping container. Viewers could see that we cared about their high-value material. Another indirect message was that we ran our business so tightly we felt it was worth creating a process even for a basic task like shipping.

Creating business processes accomplishes two things: (1) it makes whatever you're focusing on more successful and efficient, and (2) it communicates the importance of the process. That importance is evident to employees, investors, partners, vendors, and, most of all, customers. Everyone who comes into contact with your company will encounter aspects of your business that have processes. Make those processes visible and important by ensuring everyone carries them out the same way every time.

For employees, the efficiency and seriousness they see in the process design generates pride in their work. The occasional breakdown produces innovation to enhance efficiency of the working process. Nothing makes employees feel more in control and empowered than knowing their work positively impacts the company. One of the most-cited reasons employees are dissatisfied at work is the feeling that they have no impact, that they are "just a cog in someone else's machine."

Outside stakeholders, such as bankers, investors, vendors, and even family members of employees, will learn from observation that you are thoughtful about efficiency, value, cost control, employee retention, paying your bills, and so on. This creates respect, which translates ultimately to better financial terms and willingness to work with you, further increasing employee retention. No one wants to work with the less-respected company.

Customers will learn that you are diligent and standardized, and that thought and energy go into how you operate. In the customer's mind, this translates to value. If it were easy, everyone could do it, and by creating a process you indirectly demonstrate it's not easy to do what you do so well.

Your sales process is the first of your processes your customer will see.

SALES PROCESS

Most effort in business is typically spent finding and securing customers, preferably ideal customers who will repeat, receive higher value by working with you, and recommend and refer you. Without a sales process, businesses take any customer who buys, or chase prospects who will never buy.

In the previous chapter, we focused a lot on a sales process that recognizes that the customer must complete a journey to buy from you. It's their journey—you are inviting them to ascend each step until you close the deal. Understanding this, you will develop a set of actions of your own to help them make those steps up—and help you determine where they are in the journey so you can help more. What follows are a few tools you can add to your internal operations to make your sales process more efficient. Think of these as tools to help you determine how well your sales process works to feed the machine.

MANAGING CUSTOMER RELATIONSHIPS

A well-developed sales process mirrors the company's self-image: as an organization that intends to scale and grow as a well-managed business, which is proactively designed as opposed to ad hoc and reactive. A solid sales process is successful in bringing business primarily from ideal customers, and at eliminating time and effort wasted on nonideal customers. Such a process is repeatable and teachable. When the process is not followed, observable errors and failures occur. Working out of sequence, on gut instinct, or by relationship signals (based on rapport rather than established credibility, for example) is the classic mistake of a salesperson not following a process.

Many companies use customer relationship management (CRM) applications to manage their leads, prospects, and sales opportunities. Salesforce.com is one of the bigger players in the CRM business, for example, but there are many—some are appropriate for startups and smaller companies, some for large businesses with large accounts. Some CRM applications can be set up to map the stages you use to define potential customers as you move them toward buying from you. There are many names for stages in sales books—and in CRMs!—but for simplicity I'll illustrate the stages a customer must pass through using four of the most common terms: *suspect*, *prospect*, *qualified*, and *ready to close.*

A *suspect* is usually a potential customer you think may be a good fit, but who is unaware or minimally aware of you. A *prospect* is a potential customer who has made a personal connection between their problem and your possible solution. A *qualified* prospect meets your criteria as someone you can certainly help. And someone *ready to close* understands how your solution will solve their problem and what value or impact that will bring to them.

If you map these back to the customer's journey, you can identify suspects as unaware or aware, prospects as personally interested or at least understanding what you offer, qualified prospects as having a problem and presenting an identifiable and quantifiable opportunity, and those ready to close as the ones with whom you've crafted and discussed a valuable solution.

Your company might work with more, or even fewer, stages. For example, if your company offers a well-understood service or you are unique enough to be well-known in your market, you might get many leads through inbound marketing and decide they come in at the prospect stage. Within each stage, your internal sales process should define milestones that must be achieved to move forward. These allow your sales team and their managers to identify errors or breakdowns in the process.

At the suspect stage, the milestones help identify when to

convert a suspect to a prospect. For example, a suspect accepting a meeting with you might trigger the conversion. At the prospect stage, your salespeople might have to meet your process's qualifying milestones to move the prospect to qualified—defined problem, urgency, decision process understood, and so on.

Most of the gap analysis will take place at the prospect and qualified stages, when it is the salesperson's job to ensure that the potential customer meets all the requirements to become a good customer. All these milestones can be configured into most modern CRM applications. The milestones serve as prompts to salespeople learning your process, and they also help managers track the effectiveness of the process.

If you do not establish and adhere to a sales process, customers will sense that you are operating loosely, and they may devalue your product or service. Your employees will be less trusting of management and the sales team, because they'll feel burdened with small, unexpected, and unplanned orders from less-than-ideal customers. They will feel management does not have control of the business. And sales reps will leave because they lack support from your company in order to be successful.

DEVELOPING YOUR SALES OPERATIONS

Processes differ from business to business, and it takes time to develop yours and ingrain it into your business. You need to track the effectiveness of your system and have the ability to improve it. If you are beginning to set up your sales process, following are some tips for managing it operationally—in other words, using tools and systems to run your process efficiently. Don't try to do all of this at once, but remember that the goal of managing the handling of sales is to establish consistency and accountability within your team.

1. You will need a customer relationship management system. CRM applications are designed partly as databases for leads and customer interactions, but also as tools to assist salespeople and their management in following a process. You might, in the early stages of developing your sales operations, use spreadsheets to track a suspect to a prospect to a qualified sales opportunity to a closed customer. Once you're tracking a large number of leads, this will become unwieldy and it might be time to consider buying into a CRM application.

2. Assuming you have already done some work with understanding who your ideal customer is and what they care about, establish a list of qualifying criteria. These serve to exclude nonideal customers and to keep your sales team honest. Have they really established that the customer is willing to pay for the solution? I recommend you establish three to five criteria that describe a qualified prospect, and make sure each can be answered with a definitive "yes" or "no" when a sales representative is asked if their prospect meets the standard.

3. Work on your process in a flowchart format. For every branch point, fill in a path. Otherwise, your process will have dead ends where the salesperson never follows up properly, or endless loops where meeting after meeting fails to generate a proposal or quote.

4. Track your success rate or conversion rate at every stage. Knowing these key numbers allows you to set goals. For example, how many suspects should a salesperson expect to exclude before reaching a solid prospect? You will be able to develop actions to take at each stage to improve the conversion rate, and you will also know what your salespeople must work on to close the number of customers you need in order to make bank.

5. Focus on what is called *lead flow*. This means no suspect or prospect spends too much time waiting to be converted—your sales process drives action and keeps things moving. It's not uncommon for companies to accumulate many raw leads and for the sales team to spend all their time working only on qualifying late-stage prospects and trying to close sales. Meanwhile the early leads or suspects languish, contact information is out of date, and soon you have a database that offers you no benefit. The whole idea of having a process is to measure throughput. A dead lead is not just junk in the drawer—it actually clogs up your process.

6. Work with your salespeople and marketing team together on your sales process. Make goals, actions, and results visible to everyone. Remember, the purpose of marketing is essentially to find great suspects who are most likely to convert to prospects. Your salespeople must work the process and contribute to continuous improvement. A sense of ownership among the team betters the process in the long run.

MANAGEMENT

Wouldn't it be great if everyone just did what they were assigned to do and left you alone to work? Instead, most business owners share an experience of their staff that looks something like this: they want you to answer questions all the time, they do things you need to correct, they work on things you didn't ask them to do, they fight with one another, they gripe and complain, they ignore opportunities to take any initiative, they always want exceptions and make excuses, and they're half as productive as the staff you'd imagined. On top of that, they're angry with you.

A good friend in a corporate management position tells me that someday he's going to write a book titled *Managing*

Angry People. Management is a valuable skill and a necessary evil all at once. Managing effectively makes for a more productive and happier staff, more effective teams, a better hiring process, longer employee retention, and the emergence of some individuals as contributors and leaders. Management does not, however, save you from trouble, bad apples that spoil the bunch, unexpected events that disrupt your plans and strategies, and having to fire people. In short, managing is a hard job, and that difficulty is underappreciated.

Experts are naturally most comfortable in the role of technician—being the best at delivering to their customer. Those trying to be entrepreneurs—like you, the reader—see the need to create a company, and so usually become comfortable with being in charge. But giving orders doesn't make one an effective manager, nor make employees happy or prevent conflict. There's more to managing than deciding and commanding.

If you have come to the point of having to manage a staff—in addition to administering the company operationally and financially, and also managing all the sales and customers—I will bet dollars to donuts that managing employees is your most hated responsibility. It's time, once again, to grow as a businessperson.

Various sources have different lists of essential management skills, but they generally break down into these seven categories:

- Interpersonal skills
- Communication and motivation
- Organization and delegation
- Forward planning and strategic thinking
- Problem-solving and decision-making
- Commercial awareness
- Coaching and mentoring

These are not all that much help in answering the question, "What does it take to be a good manager?" It should be obvious that interpersonal skills are needed to understand and communicate with direct reports. Similarly, managers should always possess planning and strategy skills. Perhaps your management team members would like a copy of this book?

To understand not just the skills needed but how to be effective, focus on getting the most out of employees while minimizing the cost and time impact of conflict. The single most important thing a manager can do is communicate with clarity. Clarity, for a successfully managed team, means every person on the team understands three things: (1) what we do and why it is valuable to the company, (2) what I do individually to contribute, and (3) how I measure my impact. Employees' motivation in their work comes from knowing they are important (and how) and that, if they perform well or improve something, it will be noticed and appreciated.

> Overcommunicating is critical. Document everything as well. It doesn't matter if you've said something offhand, criticized, praised, or set an objective. What you think you said is not necessarily what they heard. Patience is a huge virtue for a manager.
>
> Laura Browne
>
> CEO, Covalent Bonds

Not every person is motivated all the time. In their best-selling business book, *The Oz Principle: Getting Results through Individual and Organizational Accountability*, authors Roger Connors, Tom Smith, and Craig Hickman describe how often we humans fall into the trap of victim mentality, which is characterized by a feeling of lack of control, a feeling that we are just doing what we're told and have no real impact with our work. Rather than ascribing this victim trap to an individual's personality, the authors suggest that it happens to everyone at times, and the way to combat this loss of motivation is to clarify roles and accountabilities. If every employee knows their contribution and how it is measured, they are more likely to feel in control of their impact.

If a hire is stuck in the victim role and cannot find a way out, strongly consider firing the employee. You are responsible for clarity, not for keeping people happy. A victim on your team can do a lot of damage to the effectiveness of other staffers and to your effectiveness as a manager.

Managing according to clarity sometimes seems like a lost art. And it is an art, or at least a skill, which requires careful thought and action. It's not compatible with a reactive or shoot-from-the-hip management style. In the modern workplace, employee motivation is expected to come from salary, position on the job ladder (usually about seniority, not skills or responsibilities), and accruable vacation time. But these are corporate policies, not manager actions.

As a manager, a good place to start is by helping each report know the metrics they should track—and you will track—that tells whether they're getting results that contribute to company goals. Many companies try to simplify this to one or two "key numbers" for each employee or job function. It's not much of a motivator if an employee doesn't know how missing, meeting, or improving on their number contributes. Your main objective in management is cohering your team around the idea that if everyone is achieving their goals, the team succeeds and the company prospers...and recognizes employees' performance.

Organization and delegation are skills often learned through the example of mentors and senior managers, passed on as your junior leaders take on management responsibilities. If you are not well organized, and if you are not capable of extending trust and commitment to delegate responsibilities to others, your team has no example that helps them. New managers need an example for how to organize their resources within the company model. They need a model to demonstrate that they are not judged on their ability to make every decision, but on their ability to empower others. Many inexperienced managers are not personally organized at the outset, feeling a lack of control that makes it challenging for them to delegate. They may come from a corporate culture that promotes people to management level as a reward, rather than based on skills. A culture of effective management is established from the top down.

I experienced this in the first large pharmaceutical company I worked for, the giant Pfizer. When I arrived just ahead of the 1990s, Pfizer was not so big—perhaps number twenty on the list of large drug companies. At my entry level I was a lead scientist, four levels below the CEO. When I left the company in 1998, Pfizer was on track to becoming the largest drug company in the world, and I had been promoted up four levels. By this time, I was fourteen steps down the ladder from the CEO. Achieving "management" status had become a reward for seniority, and the result was usually mediocre management.

A manager draws on their skillset to accomplish their job, which is to make the company more productive. A successful manager does the following: (1) increases productivity, (2) improves quality, and (3) decreases production costs. A manager's effectiveness should be evaluated on their ability to do all three. Decreasing costs can be easy, but doing so as the sole focus usually results in decreased productivity. Similarly, if a manager tries to increase output by simply demanding more and more, team members will eventually leave, resulting in increased costs and other negative impacts. Therefore, a manager's key numbers must reflect the goals: productivity, quality, and costs.

The problem-solving and decision-making skills needed to increase efficiency require a roadmap. Decisions should be made in alignment with the company's goals and strategy—near-term and long-term objectives. If you don't enfranchise your future leaders or junior managers with your objectives and the ability to achieve them, they will have to come to you for everything. Sadly, this is exactly the way many organizations operate. Too few managers learn the value of clarity and performance metrics.

Commercial awareness refers to the ability of managers to develop strategy and make decisions with the company. If they are not part of determining, monitoring, and adjusting company strategy and goals, they will not be able to succeed. Your team must develop a business success mindset and make decisions based on metrics that help them achieve their goals. To do this, team members must be part of the development of those metrics, which should be kept up to date and openly available to be acted upon.

Coaching and mentoring are interpersonal skills that committed individuals can learn if they realize how important these can be to success. Too often, these receive no more than lip service. Consider assessing management skills and behaviors, including emotional intelligence, of all your managers and leaders, including yourself. A lot of wisdom is packed in this simple phrase: *know thyself!*

As you grow, and find that certain team members are leading others, pay attention to their abilities not just as experts but as managers. Knowing the skillsets and gaps of all managers and potential managers, and taking action based on that knowledge, helps you to foster better leaders, make wise promotion decisions, and uncover employees dedicated to improvement.

I continue here on a cautionary note, because I've noticed a blind spot, a common mistake that has cost me and others. (I've worked with two other founders who made exactly the same mistake.) I hired a top-notch laboratory scientist from a big corporation. It was clear from the beginning that this person could solve problems, repair equipment, and develop new experimental methods—the skills of three scientists. I became dependent on them, and gave them raises and other rewards.

They were ambitious and wanted to manage employees, so as my company grew, I gave them responsibility for managing a team of scientists. All seemed good for a while, but they kept demanding more and even issued veiled threats to quit if I didn't continue to find ways to reward them. After I sold my company and left, I spoke with several employees who had resigned, and they were more candid with me than they had been while I was behind the CEO desk. My so-called star manager had actually been a huge liability, harassing young employees and manipulating reports. I feel awful to this day that I failed my staff, and I know this cost me customers and good team members. It has been a painful mistake to admit.

Entrepreneurs carry a lot of risk and keep many balls in the air at once. It's sometimes too easy for a clever employee to convince you they're essential, especially if they do things you don't want to do, like repair equipment. In small companies, offering a management position as a reward for someone's effectiveness in a nonmanagement role can be a catastrophically bad idea. The only way to avoid this trap is to know that it exists. Treat management skills as important and essential—much more valuable than technical skills as your company grows.

CUSTOMER SERVICE

Considering the common definition of the term *ideal customer*—one who repeats, pays more (gets greater value from your work), and refers or recommends—it might be assumed that more companies would adopt ongoing customer service as part of their business process.

In some industries this is common. Software-as-a-service, or SaaS, companies (such as Salesforce.com) learned to pay attention to the customer experience of subscribers after noticing low retention rates on annual contracts. In this and many other industries, it's easy for a competitor to offer similar features and lure customers away with lower prices.

Subscription software makers realized quickly that unless they stayed in contact with clients and provided support, updates, and care, they could lose to a "common features" pitch. How easy would it be for a competitor to get your customer to try their product or service—even by extending only the same offerings? After all, without trying the competitor's offer, your customer has no way to differentiate. By making it clear that the customer will lose something in discontinuing services with your business, you can create a deterrent to their jumping ship.

It's possible your customers are subscribers in the same way SaaS companies make money from renewable contracts. But for many businesses, delivery to the customer is effectively the end of the transaction. As a smart founder, you will benefit from creating a great experience that keeps customers aboard or coming back for more. Huge returns are to be gained by paying attention to delivery and response. You can make it unappetizing for your customer to defect for an alternative.

If you deliver a service or product, these components of your customer's experience are worth examining:

- Timelines (match between promise and actual time to deliver)
- Packaging
- Supporting material
- Results reporting
- Labeling
- Shipping and shipping support (response to shipment issues)
- Guarantees
- Terms and conditions (usually spelled out in a services agreement or as a supplement to the proposal)
- Email sequences alerting customers to the finish line, shipping, their next steps
- Tidy records of completion and delivery for reference in the event of an issue
- Wrap-up meetings or calls with customers
- Salesperson follow-up (right after delivery or after an appropriate period)
- Customer surveys
- Communications process for support

Using CRM applications, calendars, and email automation, many of these can be automatic and consistent—or you can at least remind staff when it's time to carry out a step in your customer experience process. To develop your program for customer delivery, look at every moment from the time you complete the work. Look from the perspective of what happens next for you, and also at what the customer sees from their point of view. Communicate these two factors through action and deed: (1) that you have it all under control (process, automation, and consistency), and (2) that your attention to detail is extremely high.

These will cause the customer to think that changing providers might be a bad idea. Their new source might not be as sharp as you are. A lack of attention to detail and consistency suggests that quality standards aren't high. And, if your customer decides to try out the competition, chances are very good that the attention to detail won't be up to par, and your work will provide a strong contrast.

My last company offered many services, and some proposals were complex. However, we offered some small commodity projects that were easy for us and expensive for customers, and these had adequate profit margins. Delivery and reporting were the same for all projects—detailed reports describing methods and results to customers, branded labeling, careful packaging, and overnight shipping.

Some of our customers had relationships with other contractors who offered similar services, but when they sent work to us to try us out, they switched to my company. We asked why. One showed us the half-baked reports from other providers. They contained little detail: a copy of the instrument-generated result (a graph) and an operator's calculation (handwritten in pen on the graph) of sample purity percentage—one page with a picture and a written number, no description, no method, and no other indication of the work's reliability.

We didn't necessarily do the work any differently from the other companies, but the way we returned results and material to the customer was visibly distinctive. Detailed reporting of methods, observations, deviations, and corrections is the standard among careful scientists. It's not strictly required in research work (as opposed to the documented work required by the FDA, for example), but adhering to a standard format suggesting a higher level of care positioned us favorably with customers. One customer told me, "Your numbers are always spot on, much closer to the actual results than the other guys." Whether this was true I never knew, but I know our reports helped create that impression!

Over the years, several of our top twenty customers were companies that used only our simplest commodity services, yet they were so loyal that they sent us hundreds of samples—for our fee of $2,000 to $5,000 each.

THE HR DEPARTMENT

As mentioned previously, I have reasons for placing human resources within operations rather than treating this function as administrative or clerical.

The role of HR in a company is to reduce costs and improve efficiency by optimizing the human resources required. This is not functionally different from setting up a lab or a manufacturing floor to provide optimal equipment in an efficient layout and keeping it in reliable condition. HR should be process driven. In the technical world, much of the hiring will be of staff concerned with production and delivery, and in any business, people are central to success. A business needs the right people operating together with minimal conflicts and bottlenecks, and you want investment in those people to pay off.

Everything in business is people oriented. Customers and employees are equally important. Just as you lose money through poor sales efforts, you will lose money by hiring the wrong people—or losing the right ones.

Create three consistent and executable HR processes: (1) hiring, (2) records management, and (3) termination procedures. All three are valuable for compliance with state and federal laws, and implementing them helps you communicate to your employees and others that you treat everyone the same.

HIRING PROCESS

Hiring for production and delivery roles—those that carry out the projects and produce your products and services—is relatively easy for us experts. Within our niche, we understand at a detailed level the work that has to be delivered to our customers. We can usually identify the key skills needed to fulfill any role. One job of a hiring manager is to look for those key skills in the candidate. Hiring based on skills—"Are you trained in Microsoft Excel?"—might seem like a yes-or-no question.

But consider the possibility that there's more to hiring technical staff than verifying on-paper skills. Scientists and engineers are good at identifying core skills and knowledge, so you and your team will probably decide a candidate is credible—or uncover a bluff—in the first few minutes of an interview. What will you do with the rest of the time? You might consider whether the candidate cares enough about your goals to fit in as an inspired team member.

Three things are important: (1) alignment with values and beliefs, (2) whether they care enough about the job to sell themselves to you, and (3) what energizes them. Whatever interview format you create, give your interviewing team the tools necessary to explore these factors.

- **What are their values and beliefs?** It's not that you care about a perfect fit—you're looking for conflicts. If, for example, you value generosity, you might say, "Tell me about a time when you solved a problem for someone. Why did you choose to jump in?" They might answer in a work or personal context, but either way you're looking for a candidate who contributes because they can or want to, not because they are required or seek a reward.
- **Do they care about the job?** The most obvious way to

understand if someone cares about *this* job (as opposed to *a* job) is to determine whether they researched you and your company before coming in. I'm always surprised by the number of candidates who fail to do this. I prefer those who ask questions about what they uncovered or didn't understand, or ask me, "Why is this position important to your company?"

- **What energizes them?** A simple way to get a candidate talking about what gets them jazzed is to ask, "What caught your eye about what we do that you feel excited about working on?" If they can't springboard from the word "excited" to describe *personal* interest in the work, they are not likely to be passionate about employment with you.

In the first five years I fired more people than I hired. Most often, it was due to a lack of culture fit. Some people couldn't adapt as we grew; some were bright but not good team members. We learned to evaluate culture fit in the interview process. We write down a description of our culture so we're forced to describe it, to ourselves and others.

We look primarily for helpers. Does the person exhibit an attitude of willingness to help others (team members, customers, etc.)? This trait is packed with other good traits underneath. Then as long as they have technical competency, we can grow them into a high-impact team member.

I personally look for their life experiences. For example, if they grew up on a farm, that tells me they can do tough jobs and see the value of grinding when the goal is worth it.

Dr. Joseph Simpkins

Founder, Virscidian Inc.

RECORDS MANAGEMENT

A huge responsibility of human resources is management of your employee records, to ensure operational integrity of your company. HR should plan, codify, test, and fine-tune your records management, compliance, cultural orientation and touchpoints, performance management, interviewing, onboarding, training, promotion, and termination procedures. HR departments—or HR processes, if you don't have a department—must be designed to make the company successful, just like every other aspect of operations.

In large corporations, HR departments often seem bureaucratic, led by execs and managers whose job is basically to protect management from being distracted by problems. HR procedures are often designed to protect privacy and to isolate personal lives and relationships from those at work, and focusing HR policy only on these things may seem off-putting to some employees. However, attention to your HR processes can help you find better employees, keep them employed longer, and create a culture where no one feels excluded. This ensures growth and success, just as much as efficiency in providing your product or service.

There are records that must be managed for legal and compliance reasons associated with hiring and termination, including identity documents, job applications, credit checks, past history, reference letters, signed agreements, performance issue records (unfortunately), and termination documents. Privacy and security of these are important, and failure to properly manage records leaves you, the employer, vulnerable to legal action launched by unhappy former employees. In many states, past abuses by companies have resulted in employment laws that put the burden of proof in a dispute on the employer rather than on the employee. Despite griping by employers when the rules side with workers, these rules are usually in place for valid reasons.

It's worth mentioning that today it's not at all unusual to

have employees who reside in different states, and employment laws and compliance differ from state to state. Whether you have a field sales rep on the other side of the country or you're based in the Boston area and have staff who live in New Hampshire, Rhode Island, Connecticut, and Massachusetts, you face the burden of multistate compliance with employment law.

TERMINATION PROCEDURE

Termination—and I don't mean when a valued employee retires with a gold watch—is unpleasant at best. Depending on the circumstances, you might feel anger, loss, fear…or relief. The employee may feel resentful and humiliated or relieved and anxious to move on. Regardless, terminating someone from their position must be done with care.

Most legal complaints workers file are to allege wrongful treatment or wrongful termination. If you fail to keep proper records regarding issues or complaints as they occur while the person is in your employ, or if your system of record keeping and records management is sloppy and not defined properly, you will likely lose in a litigious conflict. Wrongful treatment claims often result in settlements in the hundreds of thousands of dollars, and a small-business owner usually cannot survive a blow of that magnitude. It is not uncommon for us to make mistakes individually with coworkers and employees, but to fail to consistently manage the HR processes in your company so that everyone is treated fairly and equally? That's a business mistake you *can't* afford and *can* avoid.

As experts in a technology or a science, we are tempted to look at our delivery process as the core of our business operation. You can, and should, apply your analytical mind and thoroughness to all other critical aspects of your operations to ensure your company's sustainability and long-term growth.

KEY TAKEAWAYS FROM CHAPTER 12

- Business operations is so much more than the process of delivering a product or service to a customer. Operations encompasses everything you can design to create a smoothly running company, from sales operations to your HR processes.
- The design of operational functions affects your efficiency, your employees, your customers, and outside agencies with whom your business interacts. Smoothly running operations result in fewer costly problems, happier teams, and easy compliance with rules and laws. They are reflected in customer satisfaction and your brand strength, too.
- Any operational task that will be repeated—hiring and training new employees, making your product, following up on a sale—can be designed as a process. Consistency pays big dividends, so designing, codifying, monitoring, and ingraining your business processes are worth a lot of your attention. Don't fixate on the process that produces your product or service—bring your attention to *all* of your business processes.

CHAPTER 13

FINANCIALS AND METRICS

Accounting was discussed in a previous section of the book. You hoped it was over, didn't you? I know, you don't find looking at your company's finance books to be fun or interesting or even particularly useful. You have an accountant and a bookkeeper keeping an eye on finances. You've figured out these are necessary because of the following:

1. You must comply with laws, such as a state requirement that your company file an annual report.
2. You must file company tax returns.
3. Your company must not run out of money.

You might even get useful advice from your financial people every now and then, such as, "You should lease that machine, because buying it will drain your cash reserve." Not understanding the financials might make you feel a little foolish or inadequate. But *understanding your financials will help you grow*.

This is the final chapter in the Growing section of this book. If you have operations and sales running, with processes in place and a team that manages these effectively, you have cov-

FINANCIALS AND METRICS · 233

ered two of the Four Value Signals that are the indicators of a mature company that has sustainable value far beyond its founder's expertise. The third value signal is financial strength, and this chapter provides essential knowledge for attaining it.

You can track just a few numbers from your financial statements to get better performance and revenues. You can use your balance sheet to set goals to increase the value of your company. More value gives you more leverage with banks, investors, and vendors. Leverage allows you to more quickly react to opportunities and grow even more.

This chapter shows you how to do this, but I warn you in advance that it requires you to understand your financial statements—not to the degree an accountant does, but quite possibly more than you understand right now. And it requires you to regularly dedicate time to review them.

> I didn't know anything at the beginning about the business side, including financials. Part of the reason I took on a couple of partners was because I didn't feel comfortable. One of my partners already had a part-time CFO, and I would corral him for a couple of hours every time he came in. We started off with him just teaching me to understand the P&L (profit and loss), the income statement.
>
> It's not that hard, but it required a little commitment. I mean, we all went to university; we learned how to learn. This wasn't any different.
>
> Dr. Robert Suto
>
> Founder and CEO, Xtal BioStructures

METRICS

There are only six actions you can take in business that will affect profits. That's it—six things you can do. Suppose you're profitable, and the way to get more profit is to find more customers.

Only two factors determine the *number of customers* you have: (1) your *number of leads*, and (2) the *rate at which you convert* them to customers…

number of leads × conversion rate = number of customers

Very simple—either more leads, or a higher conversion rate, equals more customers. You can act to get more leads, say, by attending a trade show to collect business cards. You can increase your conversion rate by offering a deal resulting in some increase in your number of customers. There are things you can do to change the leads or the conversion rate, but you can't *do* customers. They come to you as the result of your actions.

You can increase revenue, and assuming your sales are profitable, this increases profits. Revenue is a function of the number of customers, as a result of your sales actions—but you can also take action to increase the revenue garnered from customers:

number of customers (result) × number of sales/customer (actions) × average \$/sale (actions) = revenue (result)

This should make sense to you. If you increase the number of times a customer buys, for example, by running quarterly promotion campaigns, or you increase the average value of each sale perhaps by offering an add-on or extra service, revenue increases. Again, revenue isn't the action—you must *act* and then revenue increases as a result.

Profit is simply the amount of revenue you get minus the expenses of earning that revenue. You can reduce expenses to increase profit. There are two kinds of expenses: (1) *cost of goods* (what it costs to produce your product or service) and (2) *operating expenses* (what it costs to operate the company). You can act to reduce either, and the result is an increase in profit:

$$\text{revenue (result)} - \text{cost of goods (actions)} = \text{gross profit (result)}$$

$$\text{gross profit (result)} - \text{operating expenses (actions)} = \text{net profit (result)}$$

You might find a less expensive parts supplier, for example, to reduce your cost of goods. Or decrease operating expenses—negotiate with your landlord or turn down the office heat at night—and thereby achieve the result of higher profits.

Number of customers, revenues, and profits are results that businesses often track. Such metrics immediately reveal your company's growth or contraction. The numbers don't show you *why* they are rising or falling, but they give you a read on the health of your business. They are most valuable when measured in context with the prior period or a string of periods.

Some refer to results as "lagging indicators" because they show you what happened after it happened. A "leading indicator" is something that reflects the action, not the result. The number of leads per month, for example, is a leading indicator—in most businesses, contacting more leads results in more customers.

Most owners want to see results improve over time, so looking at results month over month makes sense. Getting real-time or even more frequent updates on these key results is usually not possible—just like you pay your bills monthly, so do customers. Retail businesses might report weekly or daily totals, but monthly reports make more sense for many companies. A trailing twelve-month chart of income and expenses tells a lot about trends and their directions. As pointed out, if you do not receive and review your twelve-month income statement every month, you're missing an opportunity as an owner.

You can track all kinds of results. The trick is to determine which are most valuable to you in understanding whether your strategies are working. If you've developed a strategy to increase sales, you might monitor the total value of accepted contracts. This gets you closer to real-time performance than looking only at revenue received. The goal is to use your metrics to understand what will improve performance. If you double your number of contacted leads every month, and sales do not increase, your hypothesis that more contacts will result in more customers is flawed.

What items can you act on to improve performance—maybe conversion rate or average contract value? Once you've observed a relationship between an action and a result, try to improve the result by changing the activity level. Tracking activity metrics helps you improve performance. These are leading indicators, sometimes called key performance indicators (KPIs). When you choose to monitor a KPI, aim to understand whether or not an objective is being met or a plan is working as intended. Unless something goes wrong elsewhere, improving performance improves results. It's great to learn that your average price per quote is increasing, but only if you know the acceptance rate for your quotes is not decreasing!

Good managers use KPIs to optimize team performance. The ratio of activity to output is key in any department. If your managers are not driving to improve this, they are not performing. Help them understand that output is measured by results that you, the owner, are monitoring—and then share these results with your managers. Help them develop a list of meaningful activity indicators they can use to improve results.

INCOME STATEMENT METRICS

Many of your key results can be found on your company's income statement. Also called the profit and loss statement, or P&L, the income statement is the easiest of the three standard financial statements to understand.

The top portion is *income*—your revenue or sales. It can be broken down into income from products, services, or markets for finer granularity. If you launch a new service and want to watch it gain traction in the market, break out that service on its own income line. If you sell one service to two markets, break those out onto separate lines. Although any revenue source can be tracked, it only makes sense to separate sources of revenue if you have plans or actions in mind to improve each line. A convenience store might track gasoline and sundries sales on different lines but probably would not separate sales of chewing gum from that of chips.

The next section is usually called *cost of goods sold* (COGS), or perhaps *cost of sales* or something similar. These expenses are directly related to producing and selling the product or service—such as parts and materials or shipping and packaging. Most companies lump similar expenses together, but again the individual line items vary from company to company, and owners are free to break out expenses they want to track for strategic reasons. When you subtract the cost of goods from income, you get gross income, also called *gross profit* or *gross margin* (margins are usually expressed as a percentage, while profits are tracked in dollar amounts). If one of your objectives is to decrease costs to produce a service, thus improving its profitability, tracking gross margin is the results metric that will help you.

The last section of your income statement includes operating expenses, often just called *expense*. Operating expenses include everything it takes to keep the company operating, regardless of whether production is happening or if income is coming in or not. Salaries and facilities costs are often the biggest expenses, but you'll probably see office supplies and insurance on this list as well. Subtract these from the gross profit, and you get *net profit*. Net profit is what the business earned. It's also called "the bottom line."

Here are two lessons you must take home from this discussion:

1. **The purpose of a business is to generate revenue.** All your strategic efforts are to secure more customers and sell more to them. Reducing expenses is not a strategy, it's just an occasional activity of the responsible business owner. Your performance, which is the outcome of your strategies, is seen strictly in revenues. Did you increase revenue from one of your sources or not?
2. **Once you've determined which results to monitor, monitor them.** Share the metrics with employees, or at least with managers, because they need to know where their actions have an impact.

Your bookkeeper should provide a monthly income statement, and you must compare each current month with the past twelve months. For this to happen, you must quickly get all income and expense data to your bookkeeper—as close as possible to the moment money came in or went out. Management of your company based on financial information takes a little effort. Once you have the systems down and are used to looking at your twelve-month income statement, watch the key results: total revenue, gross profit, total expenses, and net profit. Do you see trends or unusual variations? Are there seasonal trends? Does the trend in any line reflect a result you're trying to achieve? Or does a trend point to something you could improve? That's tracking performance.

Associate your actions with their effects. Pay attention to *when* things happen—a new product launch should be followed by an uptick in revenue for that product. Is the time lag longer than expected? Maybe there's a billing cycle issue, or marketing needs to target the customer more directly. Perhaps your hypothesis about the product's value to the market was wrong—if you can't move the numbers, you may have to kill the offering.

Developing meaningful KPIs and understanding their effects probably also takes some time. Refinement is often necessary to make sure you're measuring the factors most important to you. But even early in your company's life cycle you need to know how to use financial data to understand performance. Wisdom says that what gets measured improves. By paying attention to the results of your attempts to increase performance, you zero in on their success or failure, and can adjust or redirect. Creating a culture around measurement and improvement results in greater success, and if everyone feels a part of that success and learns to track it properly, this generates excitement among your team.

By the way, don't overdo the KPIs. Try to find one KPI for each function—sales, marketing, operations, and so on—and engrain it in the culture of each team. Once each team is using the metric successfully to manage, ask them to develop one or two more to help gauge the success of their annual objectives. You will create a culture where measurement drives growth and inspires people. One of my clients, working on driving sales growth in their company, settled on a single KPI—the number of initial meetings each salesperson achieved. They've been watching that single number for a year and have seen an

88 percent increase in new customer revenue. They haven't yet felt the need to develop a second KPI.

BUDGETS AND FORECASTS

Once you're able to use metrics from your income statement to track and improve performance, you'll have an early and better picture of trends. Trends are key to two of the most important business tasks: *budgeting* and *forecasting*.

Budgeting is often thought of in terms of what one wants—a new car or a vacation—but in business, it's predicting the spend on every expense line for the coming year. Knowing what you spent last year (excluding any unusual or one-time expenses), and then incorporating any known or planned changes, gives you a budget. Add in any planned new expenditures or expenses you plan to cut, and you know how much money is needed to make the budget.

Forecasting is about predicting revenue and income from your business segments. Using revenue trends, expense trends, and the budget, you can begin to predict income for the period ahead. Straight-line prediction from trends is easy, and it has the added benefit of focusing you on maintaining the status quo. Any new business initiatives represent the potential for a further increase. For any new products or services that haven't yet caught on or been initiated, you can guess—just guess conservatively, because cutting back midyear due to a shortfall is always a challenge.

THE BALANCE SHEET AND YOUR VALUE

As you plan spending around your predicted income, pay attention to your balance sheet. The balance sheet tells you where the value is in your company—often in cash, or in equipment you've bought. You can also assign value to long-term assets such as intellectual property, trademarks, and customer contracts, but these don't have monetary value except when you sell the company or take on investors. Until you're heading in that direction, it's better to leave these intangibles out of the equation.

To understand the balance sheet, think of owning your home. Your home is called a *fixed asset*—it has value, but it can't be immediately turned into cash. To buy this fixed asset, you likely made a down payment from your own funds and borrowed the rest in a mortgage loan. The portion of the house you own is called *equity*, and the mortgage is the *liability*. The asset value is the value of the house. When you first buy the house, that asset value is the purchase price—what someone like you would be willing to pay for it.

This is the fundamental value equation:

$$\text{assets} - \text{liabilities} = \text{equity}$$

The balance sheet's way of expressing company value is the same, but to make it confusing, the standard accounting practice is to balance the equation this way:

$$\text{assets} = \text{liabilities} + \text{equity}$$

Over time, you may add value to the asset (new roof or updated bathroom, for example). Your asset gains equity, but the cost of the renovation might have come from another asset (a bank account) or another liability (a loan). You hope this investment pays off in faster appreciation of your property value, or in the pleasure of using the new Jacuzzi tub.

The value of your house might also change due to outside

factors—the neighborhood becomes desirable to commuters or a new school is built nearby—and over time their costs often inflate. Home equity might also decrease as your house ages, particularly if you don't maintain it in good condition. As you pay down the mortgage liability, your share of the value (your equity) increases.

Tracking the three important terms—*equity*, *asset value*, and *liability*—is how you determine the wealth accumulating in your home. As the equity in your home increases, your personal wealth increases. The increasing value represents an asset you can use—the equity in your home can be used to borrow more money.

Several factors determine value in your home (and what you can do with it), and it's the same for your business. Business assets allow you to borrow from a bank to expand. Businesses that use some debt to finance growth grow faster than those that rely only on income. Just as accumulating wealth shows up in your personal financials and gives you the ability to, say, get a second home mortgage or a car loan at a better interest rate, increasing the value of your business gives you *leverage* with vendors and investors.

Leverage is your ability to gain advantages, getting things done more easily or at lower cost. Trust creates leverage. A track record of success creates leverage. Reputation, the faith of others, gives you leverage. And you can use it to grow faster. Any expansion—a new product or service that brings new customers and revenue—adds value. To expand, you often need to buy new equipment, add space, or hire more staff. These cost money, and leverage means easier access to money from investors or bank loans.

There is such a thing as borrowing too much. Financing company growth with too much debt decreases your company's leverage, because others will at some point start to view you as a bad financial manager. Use your balance sheet to calculate your *current ratio.* This is the ratio of current assets (cash and accounts receivable, usually) to current liabilities (debt owed within the next year). This ratio is one of the first figures a bank will look at when deciding to lend money, because it measures your ability to repay the loan. Ask your banker what current ratio is considered healthy, and aim to maintain yours at or above that level.

A similar measure is the *debt ratio*, which is the ratio of total assets to total liabilities. Carrying some debt is valuable, because you're using someone else's money to grow, but carrying too much puts you in a weak financial position. The debt ratio is also used by banks, but it's perhaps even more useful to the forward-looking business owner because it helps you gauge your risk over the next few years. Others use ratios like these to evaluate your ability to manage your company. You can do the same.

You don't have to have an eye on the balance sheet all the time, and you won't look deeply into every line to affect strategy like with the income statement. Think of these financial ratios, and the balance sheet in general, as planning tools rather than immediate performance indicators. To build your company, the book of business (customers and revenue) is of primary importance, but your ability to create and manage a valuable entity shows true strength.

CASH FLOW IS KING

The cash flow statement—formally known as the statement of cash flows—is constructed from the income statement and the balance sheet, but it focuses on timing: *when* cash is moved in or out of the business, or *when* an internal transaction happens, such as converting cash to a fixed asset by making a purchase. Let me pose this up front: most business owners do not need to look at the cash flow statement. *Whew!*

All the same, just in case you look at it, here's a quick orientation. Cash flow transactions come in one of three categories:

- Cash flows from operating activities
- Cash flows from investing activities
- Cash flows from financing activities

Operating activities are easy to spot—revenue comes in, and expenses go out. The timing is not always obvious, because on your income statement you book revenue when you send out an invoice, and the expense when the bill arrives. The cash doesn't come in until the customer pays, and sometimes we are forced to accept payment terms of ninety days or longer from desirable customers. Your vendors will insist, though, that you pay them. So even when the income statement shows plenty of money coming in, your bank account may say otherwise. Promptly send out invoices, and negotiate the best payment terms you can, but beware that receivables often don't come in as quickly as payables go out.

Investing activities reflect what you invest in the business. Buying equipment or real estate is a common investment. This can get complicated, made so by leasing arrangements and depreciation rules. Don't get bogged down, but remember that *investing activities* mostly describes the conversion of income from business or financing into fixed assets. Spendable cash is converted into hard assets needed to do business. And investing activities can go either direction—you can sell an asset, like a company truck, for cash that goes back into the company account.

Financing activities refer to debt, investor funds, and owner financing—taking money in *and* paying off obligations. Again, cash is coming in or going out. Remember that in describing the balance sheet, I suggest monitoring your current ratio and debt ratio. These help make sure your spending on equipment or other large expenditures don't consume too much cash on hand, and that your debt stays within a healthy limit. Use these balance sheet ratios at any time to see whether you're using cash and leverage in a safe way, and by doing so you can usually ignore the cash flow statement. What's important here is that you gain familiarity with the concept that revenue, profit, and cash on hand do not track along the same curve.

Imagine you enter a new business, perhaps within your current company, by adding a new product or service. It will take a little time to get ready to sell, and during this time you probably have some setup, labor, or even development and testing costs. Cash is going out the door, but revenue isn't coming in yet. When revenue eventually comes and development costs are past, the cash outflow—the bleeding—stops. Startup and development expenses decrease, and revenue increases to cover those costs. This is great—your revenues are now enough to fund production and delivery, but you're still out all those initial costs. Your bank account balances are at their lowest!

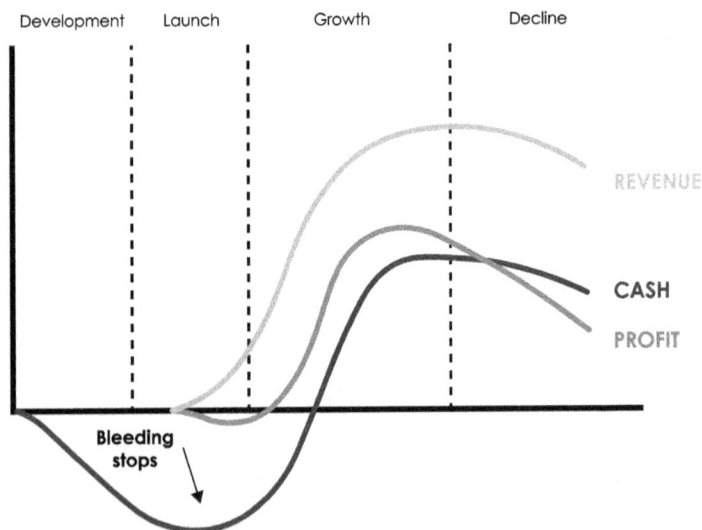

Once growth starts, revenues increase to the point where some profit is coming in. At that point cash flow turns positive, and profits start to make up the early loss. If there's enough profit, you will first replenish the bank accounts and then add to them. Profit accumulates until competition eats into your returns and you must reinvent a portion of your business to keep it growing. That's the universal business cycle.

Keep this in mind: just when you break even, you're the most broke! The cash needed to launch anything new must be anticipated (to the extent possible) and working capital reserves are needed to fund you past launch.

A smart business owner will never *plan* to deplete working capital to the point that the business is at risk of defaulting on payroll or rent. But it happens. The Great Recession of 2008–2011 caused many companies' revenues to fall dramatically for a year or longer, and those that had limited working capital closed shop or sold at a loss. Businesses run out of cash all the time, and because many owners think in profit-and-loss terms and fail to think about cash requirements, the cash drain is always a surprise. Nothing is more crushing than the sudden realization that you won't have enough to make your next payroll. With a basic understanding of cash flow, you will be in a better position to plan and protect your company.

KEY TAKEAWAYS FROM CHAPTER 13

- To understand financial statements is to make your business stronger. Financial statements don't have to be confusing and impenetrable, but instead are extremely valuable to a business owner. For example, monitoring results and trends on your income statement extracts performance metrics that help you and your team execute.

- By monitoring some key ratios on your balance sheet, you increase your company's value and leverage. Paying attention to some key ratios also helps you place limits on spending and on the amount of debt you should take on to grow your company.
- Cash flow is nonintuitive (at least if you try to understand it as an accountant) but something every business owner needs to grasp at a simple level. Because completing work, shipping a product, or starting up a new business area doesn't result in an instant cash return, you can get into trouble and run out of cash. Learning a little can help you a lot in terms of setting targets for the amount of cash to have on hand.

KEY TAKEAWAYS FROM SECTION TWO

- The art of the successful business leader is characterized by growth, where growth is defined as creating a company that is more than just the efforts of the owner. This doesn't mean you can't create a company that produces a nice living for you and some employees, but it does mean spending some of your effort working *on* the company rather than *in* the company!
- To build a company that is more than you, the owner—your expertise and hard work—you must master these three functions of a business: operations, sales and marketing, and finance and administration.
- You can measure your progress toward building that company as an independently functioning entity with value of its own. The Four Value Signals were developed in response to the question, "How do I know when I've done it?" Of course, you can use the Four Value Signals for more, such as increasing the value of your company for future sale. But that's the next section…

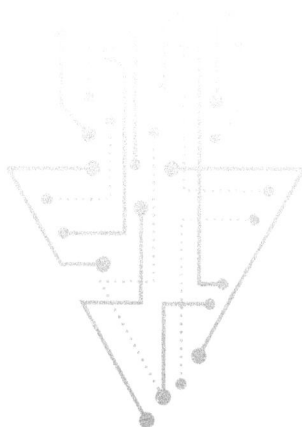

SUCCEEDING

"There are no limits to what you can accomplish, except the limits you place on your own thinking."

—BRIAN TRACY

"Success is not the key to happiness. Happiness is the key to success. If you love what you are doing, you will be successful."

—ALBERT SCHWEITZER

CHAPTER 14

MEASURING YOUR SUCCESS

The subtitle of this book, *How to Turn Your Hard-Won Expertise into a Thriving Business*, implies that success is equated with a thriving business. By my definition, a thriving business means the business runs by itself. The company's founder and its leadership have built it so systems and staff are in place that don't depend on one individual—the expert whose unique skills and drive started it all. Success, then, can be measured against the Four Value Signals—the strength of the *team*, a consistent process for finding and *profiting* from customers, healthy *financials*, and a lack of dependence on the *founder* or owner.

If you're reading this before or during the startup phase of your company, some of this discussion includes evaluating your potential for exiting when the time comes. Often this means selling or transferring your company, both of which require you to agree on its monetary value. You're probably not there yet. Still, I recommend reading this chapter for a view of the goalposts. It will give you an idea of where you're going, and whether or not you have any vision of an eventual sale. The Four Value Signals are a great way to gauge success even if you never exit.

Ultimately, you get to decide if your company has reached

the level of maturity you want. Here is a short quiz to help you gauge your progress by the Four Value Signals.

TEAM

1. Do you have leaders who are responsible for operations, sales and marketing, and finance and administration? One of these can be led by you, but only one.
2. Does each leader manage their unit according to transparent metrics? Do those metrics drive team performance?
3. Do your key leaders work together to achieve annual goals?

SALES PROCESS

1. If you, the owner, were not involved, would sales decline?
2. In addition to using basic criteria such as funding, does your sales team qualify prospects based on ideal customer profile?
3. Do your marketing program and collateral, including website, generate a sustainable and growing flow of new leads?

FINANCIAL STRENGTH

1. Are you using financial metrics as tools for company growth and forecasting?
2. Are your current financial ratios adequate to secure new bank lending?
3. How long would it take you to double your cash on hand, at current levels of business activity? This should be no more than two calendar quarters.

FOUNDER INVOLVEMENT

1. If you, the key expert and founder, were to walk away from the company for a three- to four-month hiatus, how much might revenue decline?
2. Do you manage more than one of the three primary functions of the company? These include operations, sales and marketing, and finance and administration.
3. Would a competitor buy your business if you were to vacate your position as head of the company?

Owners who achieve success by this measure are justifiably proud. Instead of gauging their value by the salary they could get in a corporate job or income as a consultant, they've built something new that accumulates value. It's natural for some to ask, "What's next? I built something valuable. Isn't that part of my personal wealth?"

You do not have to measure success this way. Maybe you genuinely enjoy your business and don't want to quit. So what if it's small, if it earns a nice living for you and your staff? Some business owners will always work in their business. Perhaps the business never grows beyond needing their expertise at the center—sort of like a consultant with a support team.

Nothing is wrong with this way of looking at a business. If you are such an owner, you've still accomplished what few do—you turned your hard-won expertise into a revenue stream. In doing so, you contributed to a family or community and to your employees' families and communities. You may have used much of this book to your advantage or learned similar lessons through your own experience. I hope this book was of some help to you.

If, on the other hand, you chose to develop your business to become independent of your expertise, this section should be valuable to you. You chose to work *on* the business instead of *in* the business. If the company you've built has achieved this level of maturity, your business has value even without you as the owner. Many owners are aware their business has stand-alone value. Maybe you've even received inquiries about whether your company is for sale.

You have three options for finishing up your adventure of starting and growing a business: (1) you can sell it, reaping a reward for the wealth you've socked away in your company's equity and continued potential; (2) you can give it away, meaning you can pass it along to someone else like a charitable donation or an inheritance; (3) you can do nothing until the day comes when you decide to close it down.

All of these are successful exits. Nothing wrong with handing down a business as family wealth, nor is there any reason you shouldn't earn a nice living for years and then retire comfortably after saying a fond farewell to your remaining loyal customers. But if you've grown to a size and degree of efficiency such that your company is now a self-supporting entity run by talented leaders with solid processes, you have built value beyond just your revenues. A smart buyer will pay for that.

I feel the most satisfying aspect of building a business is seeing it become more than the sum of its parts. It takes time and work, and the lion's share of that time and work usually comes from the owner. Your personal investment not only earned you a decent living during your years as an operator, but it also accumulated wealth for you. If your goal is to realize that wealth, whether by making it your family legacy or selling your business for a monetary return, these last couple of chapters deal with the basic components of business value to help you with the process of completing a transfer or sale of your company.

DEFINING "VALUE"

There are ways to measure whether or not your business has become an entity with inherent value. I created the Four Value Signals concept as a means of quickly determining not only the degree of the company's maturity, but also to give owners an indicator of where they can apply their efforts to develop their business to receive the greatest return.

Building value—enhancing the value of your company— of course means you can likely sell your company for more money. A $5 million (revenue) company with a solid team, a standardized process for acquiring and retaining customers, a strong balance sheet, and an owner who is not micromanaging everything will sell for more than a $5 million company that lacks these strengths.

But value means much more to you as an owner. It means leverage—people want to work with you because you have a proven track record of smart success. It means satisfaction and peace of mind, because you've built something bigger than yourself. It probably means a better life for you. It means wealth to achieve your personal goals, maybe a happy retirement or a legacy.

Increasing revenues validates your expertise and your idea. You were right all along—this idea made a successful business, and you did it well. Increasing value at transfer, liquidation, equity investment, or sale is a measure of your ability to build something beyond yourself. You'll have to measure value in your preferred type of transaction against what you think all your hard work and success is worth. For the purposes of this book, I use the most universal measure of a thing's value: whatever someone will pay you for it equals its worth.

THE IMPORTANCE OF THE VALUE SIGNALS TO A BUYER

Buyers come in different stripes. Despite their somewhat varied goals in an acquisition, all buyers will try to gauge your company's degree of sustainability. Unless they want only your company's physical assets, such as the equipment, buyers typically want to make money from operating your company, not from liquidating it.

YOUR TEAM

When experts start a company, they have a natural tendency to pour that expertise into every aspect of the business. This is rational, as founders are trying to establish their market, their positioning, and their process based on the value they intend to deliver. As we've learned, companies become truly valuable when they grow beyond their early reliance on the founder's energy, skill, and reputation. To get to this stage, the founder must stop wearing too many of the hats.

The three primary functions within any business—operations, sales and marketing, and finance and administration—need leadership independent of one another. Increasing sales pushes on operations and administration. External efforts to sell more and more effectively, if successful, require more internal resources to effectively deliver products and services. Internal growth requires financing and adds capacity, which pushes sales and marketing divisions to produce more business.

With the right leadership in these positions, future growth is limited only by the size of your market. Choosing to go after new markets is a strategic decision, and a strategy must be developed and executed. If you have strong leadership that you trust in the abovementioned trio of critical functions, your company's growth potential can be vast and indefinite.

However, some owners stop short of forming a team structure with high-achieving leaders in these positions for two reasons: (1) First, they don't know how to train leaders through delegation, mentorship, and clarity. Many owners are learning themselves how to lead! (2) Directly hiring trained leadership is expensive and risky. A mistake in hiring to fill a key position such as head of operations could be costly.

Let's assume you're reading this because you've got a solid leadership team. When you hired an experienced head of operations or head of sales and marketing, you accomplished three things:

1. You let loose the daily responsibilities of that function.
2. You created pressure on the other function (sales if you hire operations, operations if you hire sales), and that pressure illuminated weaknesses and revealed opportunities to strengthen that function.
3. You found someone with ethics similar to yours to check, validate, open up, or add to your ideas. You began building a leadership team, and you could keep each other on track.

When this new leader is a success, the salary and expenses are more than offset by the compensating growth of your business. You go on to hire leadership for the other function (operations, or sales and marketing). This probably leaves you, the owner, in charge of finance and administration. You move away from the day-to-day function and assume a more forward-looking role, working now with a competent team to set growth strategy.

No doubt you've maintained your status as the founding expert, and you're probably still in contact with key customers in your bigger accounts. But by representing yourself in the oversight role, rather than the direct delivery or management role your customers see, you've become a business leader instead of just an expert. A prospective buyer of your company will be more comfortable knowing you will eventually transition out in favor of new leadership.

SALES PROCESS

When you are the only salesperson—you the expert, you the owner—you similarly approach each sale. You have a personal style or way of selling. Maybe you're good at it and have none of the common limitations, such as asking too few questions, talking too much about money, and trying too hard to get access to higher-ups who sign off on bigger contracts. But as you build a sales team, you'll be more successful if you carve out a consistent sales process rather than allow everyone to ad-lib within their own limitations.

Selling according to a deliberate process positions you as a successful and mature business. Imagine you get an out-of-the-blue inquiry: "How much does X cost?"

You respond, "Well, that depends. Why are you asking? Tell me something about what you're trying to do." When they insist on just getting a price, you explain, "We don't work that way. Our process is to first understand your need or problem before we can give the best price. Would you like to discuss that?" This simple process garners respect from a good customer and weeds out the bad.

To get to a certain level of success, you learned to be a good representative of your company, able to sell using an approach that works well much of the time. Then you decide to hire a salesperson. They have a good track record, experience in selling similar products or services to your market, and a network of more than five thousand prospects. They have sales training from a big-name firm. Do you want them to use their process, whatever it is, or expect them to adopt yours? This is probably the first time you have faced the question of whether or not you should have a consistent sales process.

Your company's sales process is one of its greatest assets. Every person in a sales function knows the steps—how your marketing invites the right prospects, how customers are qualified, and how you develop a tailored solution. All salespeople are trained to implement your company's process of customer qualification, gap analysis, and presentation techniques. Your proposals are based on a template that begins with a description of the problem your company will solve and the value that will bring to the customer. If a new salesperson takes over an existing account, the customer experiences little change in the way you do business with them— even if they don't have the same personal history with the new representative, the process remains familiar.

In terms of value, a consistent and demonstrably successful sales process represents tight control in every aspect of the business. Operations and sales together create a customer experience that ideally generates repeat business. The sales process is how the company interacts with the outside world and continues to function as a business.

A potential buyer of your company will evaluate your sales process from a variety of perspectives, including documents, conversion rates, customer definition, lead accumulation strategies, growth rate, and customer surveys. If they see an opportunity to grow your company after they acquire it by installing their own sales process—because they view yours as limiting—they will do so. They might undervalue your company with claims that it is not performing as well as it could, with the objective to increase performance postacquisition by instituting major changes in the way your company now operates. If this happens, you profit less from the sale and lose control (or your leadership team will) after the sale closes.

FINANCIAL STRENGTH

Much of your company's financial strength is measured from the balance sheet and by examining its vulnerability to cash flow fluctuations. What does a prospective buyer—someone interested in placing a value on your business—look for on your balance sheet?

Assets. Have you used money generated by your business to accumulate assets? Maybe you own instrumentation or equipment used for manufacturing or delivering services? After depreciation (the accounting term for the loss in asset value over time), those fixed assets have a residual value. Perhaps you bought your building as a hedge against inflation, or you have vehicles or technical instrumentation. These are not only part of the value of your company, but also a start in understanding how your business runs.

At the point of negotiating a sale, you can also place a value on intellectual property, including trademarks and trade secrets, and you can value customer contracts. Your accountant can help you assign a value to these long-term assets. A blanket category for long-term assets in a business is called *goodwill,* representing a premium a buyer paid (if you sold) or would pay (if you sell in the future) over comparable prices for businesses in your industry. In some industries, goodwill even factors in *soft assets* like brand strength or even employee relations, but these usually don't apply with small to midsize businesses.

Is your equipment starting to fail, needing replacement, old technology? Or is it new and state-of-the-art? Is your building (if you own it) worth more than the value assigned to it on your books, due to a rising commercial real estate market? What would the new owner have to do to increase the capacity or profitability of your business? Remember, your buyer doesn't have to value your assets at what you list on your books!

Liabilities. If you borrowed money to buy, or leased your equipment, good for you. If those liabilities exceed your assets' value, not so good. If you're thinking of selling in the future, pay attention to your debt-to-equity ratio and try to minimize it. If you're trying to borrow money from a bank or secure an investor, make sure ratios of current liabilities (due in the coming twelve months) to current assets are low enough that you won't hit any cash flow issues in the coming year.

Equity. This is what remains after you subtract all your liabilities from your assets. Keep in mind that this is often a negative number when a company is young. Just like the equity in your home grows as you improve it and as the market rises, you will grow equity in your business by investing in the company and becoming more profitable.

Equity is the sum of the owners' and investors' contributions, the net income (profit) from the income statement, and all monies earned from the company's inception that are reinvested (retained earnings) in the company. Any profits over the history of the company that is not paid out to owners—shareholders— is by default retained in the company, and either sits in the bank or is used to acquire assets.

What is a buyer looking for? Sound money management and a clear indication that the company is in a position for continued growth. Think again of your house: if you have too much mortgage debt relative to its value, maybe because of damage or poor maintenance—maybe because of market factors that caused a decline in value of your neighborhood—this is equivalent to overleveraging your business, not staying current with technology, or failing to anticipate a change in market trend. All of these devalue your business. The business skills and financial skills you must develop in order to profitably run your business will show up in the final valuation of your company.

Financial strength must be built and managed. Some successful businesses generate just enough cash to maintain operations and pay salaries, including the owner's salary, but these will not command the greatest valuation and will be especially vulnerable in an economic downturn. Businesses that generate excess cash that can be used to add assets, reduce debt, and pay owners dividends are much more valuable—especially if their ability to generate cash is increasing. You, as the owner, must manage your business to profit—to generate cash—if you want to maximize its value.

The founder or owner. If your business depends on your being there for anything to be accomplished, whether sales, delivery, vendor negotiations, personnel disputes, hiring, or banking, it's not likely you will ever be able to leave the company. If you were to sell, the buyer would want to lock you into a legal contract to prevent you from leaving because otherwise, they would not own a functioning business. The impacts of this on your home life, family, personal goals, and health might be significant.

Most buyers don't want this any more than owners do. In fact, negotiating the eventual exit of the founding entrepreneur is one of the toughest parts of selling a company. The seller (owner) is usually willing to give the new owner some time to smoothly transition into control, but staying on past this point means the former owner is merely an employee and must defer to the new owners before making many decisions. This shift from in-charge owner to subordinate employee is not easy, often resulting in tension and an unhappy separation.

Recognizing that the owner is selling to gain an eventual exit means buyers are happiest when your company is set up to run properly—without your constant intervention. Demonstrating that you've achieved this generates a substantial increase in value. Even if you aren't selling now, setting up your business to be more independent of you means you get time to spend with family, go to the gym, take vacations—and you'll sleep better at night. You might finally get what you wanted when you started: proof that your skills and good ideas, and your devotion, could create a successful and satisfying business worthy of your pride.

If you have built a company that runs without your active managing, you minimize risks in negotiating for your exit, and you will likely get a higher offer and better contract terms besides. That is why the degree of owner involvement is considered one of the Four Value Signals.

> We planned for exit from the very beginning, although it's always difficult to know how long it will take to get there.
>
> We know what our profit target is to make us marketable. We're building the team, and processes, to make everything really efficient. As soon as we hit our targets, we're going to pivot to 100 percent sales efforts—bring on the maximum business we can handle, and then the company will be at its maximum value.
>
> If we get an offer early, we'll consider it only if it's got additional value for us—strategically or in the offer itself.
>
> At the moment, we're too dependent on my being involved all the time. If I neglect a client, it's noticeable, they get upset, and there's not enough of me to go around. I've started training my staff to do what I do, and I'm tracking client feedback more carefully. Some of the transfer of responsibility can be done with a process or a flowchart, but a lot is building experience. The team is starting to say, "We've got it; you don't need to be in the meeting." I'll know I've been successful when clients don't ask where I am!
>
> Laura Browne
>
> CEO, Covalent Bonds

KEY TAKEAWAYS FROM CHAPTER 14

- You don't have to ever exit your company. You can choose to close it down or "die in the saddle" (metaphorically, I'm sure). Whether you decide to exit or not, you can increase your company's value to you, in satisfaction or monetary return, by focusing on how its underlying value is determined.

- The Four Value Signals concept is a shorthand way of determining the degree of maturity you as owner have built into the company. The signals determine the attractiveness of your business as an asset. Its revenues, profitability, balance sheet, and other factors determine its price.

- The Four Value Signals can serve as guideposts on your journey toward building a self-sustaining company. You can use these guideposts to achieve faster growth and get greater leverage and satisfaction. If a buyer inquires, you'll be in a good position to determine whether you're ready to receive a good offer.

CHAPTER 15

EXITING

THE ENDGAME

This chapter is somewhat of an owner's manual for negotiating that sale. If you're nowhere near selling, you can read now to scope out such a situation. And then you can always return to it later!

As previously noted, you can exit your business by closing operations, transferring the business to insiders, or selling to an outsider. The latter two are more complex, particularly selling to a buyer who is not as familiar with what you've built than your family might be, for example. If you choose to just close down, you must close out client relationships, terminate your employees, sell your building or get out of your lease, and sell any equipment. Then, as some say, "Go in peace."

To transfer the company (to employees or family, most often), you set the terms and the transferees agree to them. Negotiations and disclosures often take place organically and over long periods of time, so in the end you make a deal that works for everyone and then take your terms to a lawyer to draw up documents. This process resembles selling your company, so if this is the avenue you plan to take, this chapter is worth reading. However, the transaction will likely be less complicated than dealing with an outside buyer.

But what if you receive an inquiry from a competitor, a partner, or a group you've never heard of, about your interest in selling? How do you decide whether or not to start a discussion?

BUYERS

There are three types of buyers: strategic, financial, and opportunistic. (1) *Strategic buyers* are interested in adding your business to theirs for strength. They look for businesses whose addition would result in a company with greater revenues or profits than the sum of its parts. (2) *Financial buyers* are interested in your cash flow, and they buy with the intent to maximize that cash flow as their return. (3) *Opportunistic buyers* have lots of motivations, but they are looking to acquire your business primarily as an asset they can leverage—to sell later for a profit or to operate passively as a cash source. Opportunistic buyers often look for businesses that are in distress or businesses in which the owner wants out quickly.

If you have built your business to be an asset by virtue of its expertise, technology, or process, you may find a strategic buyer who is attracted to these qualities. In my experience, expert owners often believe their specific capability has such high value that they will consider offers only from buyers who intend to use their company as a strategic asset. Strategic buyers usually pay more, because they seek the extra value creation they get by adding your capability to what they already have. But strategic buyers are harder to attract. They must see your business as unique in its capabilities, quality, and reputation. It takes time and effort to make your company maximally attractive to a strategic buyer. But that's the end goal this book has been about, to maximize the value of your business.

A financial buyer may be a good choice if you've created a highly profitable and tightly engineered business. Your company's success might have encouraged others to compete with you, so your business may not be unique or even top within your segment—your success might be more closely related to how you've managed the business. A financial buyer will add you into their organization by sharing back-office functions like accounting and HR, resulting in even greater profitability through the reduction in overhead. Private equity (PE) investors are usually financial *and* strategic buyers, who look at your growth potential within their core business segment but measure the success of their purchase based on your profitability.

An opportunistic buyer will buy your business at a discount rather than what it would be worth if its situation, or external pressures like the economy, were not negatively impacting the company. It's not unheard of for an owner to sell to an opportunist in a bad economy. I consulted with an owner who sold due to a family situation—his wife became ill, and through a business broker he was able to find a buyer whose purchase allowed him to receive much of the value he'd accumulated in his business as cash, so he could address the family need. He also retained his job, with salary and benefits, as managing director. Sometimes selling to an opportunistic buyer is a good long-term financial choice.

You are not obligated to accept any offer, and you can create a strategy to attract any type of buyer you want at any time. Knowing what types you might want, and how to identify them, is valuable to you as owner.

HOW SELLING YOUR BUSINESS WORKS

When your early business advisers talked about an exit strategy, they didn't mean, "How are you going to get out?" They meant, "How will the owners [shareholders] monetize the effort and investments, over time, that they put in to grow the company?"

After initiating your startup planning and actions, you immediately started on growth of your business. But ultimately it is about growth in value, as opposed to growing your company in physical size or revenues. If you've done most of what has been addressed in this book, you now own a company that is worth much more than when you started it. You profited from your efforts along the way by paying yourself a salary or distribution of profits, but in the end, you built a business that holds value—beyond you. Exiting, for you as a shareholder, is about pulling that value out while the company remains capable of generating value for its next owners.

The next owners may be your employees or family members, a competitor or partner company, or an investor group building a portfolio of profitable companies. Whomever the next owner will be, the process is more or less the same for you and your other shareholders, if any. The transaction is less governed by formalities when the next owners are family members, and more dictated by spreadsheets if the new owners are pure investors, but a similar process is involved nevertheless. This breaks down into two independent activities: *due diligence* and *negotiation*.

Finding a buyer can be easy if your company is obviously well-run and growing and in an industry (like many science and technology fields) where there is a lot of investor interest. You may receive unsolicited inquiries. If you've decided the time is right for you to sell and you want to encourage inquiries—and be able to rapidly judge whether they are worth considering or not—you may want to engage a business broker or investment banker to help market your company. This can be as open or as stealthy as you want—you will set the terms the broker will use to approach potential buyers and control the information you disclose in marketing your business. Think of a broker as a highly experienced and well-connected real estate agent listing your house for sale. The broker will take a percentage of the return from the sale under terms you negotiate with them.

When the buyer is an outsider (not family or employees), you'll receive an inquiry directly or through an intermediary, and it's up to you whether you want to hear more. Often to hear more, you'll have to have a conversation that reveals a little about your company's performance. Maybe you supply a very short summary of the last couple of years' financials and a balance sheet. It's not appropriate to go any further without some guarantee of serious interest in purchasing, and then only under a nondisclosure agreement (NDA).

When official steps of the sale begin, they move from less formal to more so. An early indication of interest (IOI) letter is sent to show formal interest, and it usually asks you to disclose some more financial statements and other insider information about you and your business. Following that, a more weighty-looking letter of intent (LOI) announces the buyer's intent to make an offer of a specified amount, although the amount and payment terms (payment at close of sale, milestone payments, earnouts [described below], payment in cash versus their company stock) are still somewhat amendable pending a due diligence process.

The LOI usually spells out the buyer's exclusive right to go deep in your records for a short period, usually sixty to ninety days. Expect these letters to say that any terms offered are non-binding, meaning that if the buyers don't have to be bound by what the letter says, neither do you!

Due diligence is unpleasant for many owners. The process involves digging up and copying endless records. You will feel you're supplying duplicate information in slightly different formats again and again. Your accountants and theirs will argue about the presentation of your financials, and it will seem that lawyers (theirs, of course—I know you trust your attorney!) are circling like sharks, looking for ways to take bites out of you.

Beyond the irritation and hassle of due diligence, the process distracts you from your primary job with your business. Unless you have truly created a business that runs without you, you can expect a period in which your efforts will be impaired, and revenues or profits may even drop. This performance drop can cause a buyer to adjust their offer downward.

Once due diligence is complete, and you and your buyer are in agreement on basic terms, lawyers will work on a stock purchase agreement or asset purchase agreement. Similar to a bill of sale, but usually much longer and more complex, this agreement requires your careful attention. You will probably also have to review a separation agreement or, if you've agreed to stay with the company for a time, an employment contract.

All of these will be new to you if you've never sold a company before. Owners who have worked hard to grow their companies usually have less experience in business acquisitions than do the bigger companies that are buying them. And buyers certainly will use this knowledge gap—real or imagined—to their advantage. If you feel overwhelmed or sense that you might be taken advantage of, slow down and talk to your advisers.

During these activities, you will get to know your buyer better than ever. You may not like what you see. Part of this is natural—you and your buyer have competing interests. Theirs is to acquire your business for as little investment as possible, while yours is to get out with a fat bank account. They may very well devalue elements you've developed that are unique and differentiating, products of your genius in understanding your customers' desires, brilliant concepts that no one else has thought of, great sources of pride to you and your team. Don't take the negation personally. Persevere, but be ready to walk away if your deal no longer meets the initial goals you set.

Walking away from a deal in progress is *very challenging*. You have already put time, effort, and money into this. Your business activity may have slumped a little from the distraction, and rebuilding it is not appealing. Walking away feels like a defeat. And you have begun to envision your postexit life, right? You can easily get trapped by these feelings, psychologically influenced by sunk-cost fallacies. But don't let your personal ideas of success and failure keep you from terminating a bad deal. It is very difficult to be cold and rational about your business, the years you invested in growing it, and the excitement and hope you have for the deal. The best way to avoid being trapped is to think about the possible scenario ahead of time, talk it through with your advisers, and ask them to help you remain clear-eyed throughout the process.

Here's a short summary of what to be aware of when entering a discussion of selling your company:

- Your business should be capable of running smoothly, without much contraction, for at least the three months necessary to complete a deal.
- You should get an industry benchmark and market valuation analysis, usually available from an experienced business brokerage service or investment banking group. If you have engaged a business broker, they should have a source for these reports. Benchmarking within your industry will tell you how your size, efficiency, and financials compare with

typical companies. A market valuation will give you an idea of what a fair offer for your company would be in the current market. These should be accessible for an investment of $2,500 to $5,000 without having to sign a contract with a broker. You need to know what a fair offer for your company looks like. I recommend doing this at minimum every two years, once you suspect you are big enough to achieve a profitable sale.

- Never sign any document, even a nonbinding IOI, without first having your attorney and your accountant review it. Other advisers or board members should review these documents as well. Your objective is to choose the right buyer, not just the right deal.

- Expect conflicts and treat them as business conflicts, not personal ones.

- Qualify your buyer as they are qualifying you. From where will they secure the funds to buy your company? Do they have experience with acquisitions, and if so, how much experience? Who are their outside accountants and lawyers—are they reputable?

- Expect that if due diligence is long or negotiations are sticky, you will incur additional costs. Be prepared to absorb these costs even if the deal does not close, or walk away.

- Work to determine at the LOI stage how the buyer intends to structure the deal—payment terms, timelines, your role, contractual obligations to the new owner, goals you will be asked to achieve if you stay on, and so on. Remind them that although the LOI is nonbinding, they need to be clear so you can evaluate the deal. If terms are not clear, you may receive an unpleasant surprise later.

- Protect your employees from exposure to what's going on during due diligence and negotiation. Staff members often find the idea of new ownership very destabilizing, and their work will slow down.

- Your employees will probably see a change in culture after the acquisition. Start early to understand what this will look like, and how much it is likely to affect your staff. Cultural fit means both your team and the new owners are more likely to win in the transaction.

- Think long and hard about whether, and under what circumstances, you would like to be involved under the new ownership—maybe as director of their new subsidiary, perhaps in a consulting role, or no involvement at all. Your employment contract, if you choose to stay on, should be something you can live with and enjoy.

According to a study by the accounting giant KPMG, 83 percent of merger and acquisition (M&A) deals fail to increase returns for shareholders.[5] Lawyers are often the only clear winners. Careful planning may secure a handy return for you as the seller, but would you want to walk away having failed to make the deal work as planned? There are lots of aspects to a change in ownership you can't control, but you can try to anticipate issues, refuse to engage in wishful thinking, and be honest and direct with your buyer. Recognize that the nature of the relationship during the deal is at least partially adversarial. Acknowledging that, and resolving to be open about it, increases the odds of a happy marriage.

Careful preparation on your part makes your deal happen faster and more smoothly, reducing risks. Sufficient working capital to get into a deal process reduces your financial risk. Solid due diligence and negotiating on your part, especially around fit,

---

5   Margaret Hefferman, "Why Mergers Fail," MoneyWatch, *CBS News*, April 24, 2012, https://www.cbsnews.com/news/why-mergers-fail/.

plans, culture, and the future, also limit the risks for those you leave behind: employees, customers, and partners. And good work on the Four Value Signals helps ensure you get a good return!

DUE DILIGENCE

A comprehensive due diligence checklist is included in the appendix. It was adapted from MBA program sessions that focus on M&A. Don't let it scare you. You can learn a couple of important factors just by looking over the checklist.

1. First, your buyer can, and should, ask for your full disclosure of everything that might affect the value they get from the deal. They have a right to do so, and if you want a deal, you will disclose all necessary information.
2. Second, if the buyer asks for every single item—that is, without regard to whether it is even pertinent to your company or industry—they are proceeding by checklist and not with intelligence, meaning they have little experience. This may help you decide to end the deal discussion, or it could give you a strategic advantage!

As the seller, you are likely to be at a disadvantage in the deal—hopefully, a slight one. Just as in selling your house, you're at the mercy of the buyer's willingness to complete the deal even if they find a few warts or blemishes when they take a close look during due diligence. The buyer is often bigger and more experienced at acquisitions than the small business owner. The buyer may have more cash reserves. Due diligence and legally closing a deal cost money, and once you've spent a hefty sum it may be harder for you to consider walking away even if you're having second thoughts about the sale.

Once an LOI is signed, due diligence will likely proceed. If you have concerns or must share negative information (pending lawsuits, large loans, businesses in trouble, past fines, or regulatory actions, to name some examples), it's better to share early on and discuss how you're resolving these issues. If any of these would cause the buyer to walk away, your costs will be minimized. Be assured, all your closeted skeletons will be exposed during due diligence. And if you fail to disclose until after a deal is signed, you may be subject to legal action.

OK, enough warnings—I'm sure you're in good shape to sell despite a few fully resolved past problems. So, how does due diligence actually work?

Your buyer (or your broker or theirs) sets up a secure document exchange area online, often called an e-room. They start by sending you a list of what they want you to upload to the e-room—with luck, their list won't be as lengthy as the one in the appendix. You'll promise to load everything they want within, say, two weeks. And four weeks later, you still won't be done sharing documents, because they will ask for more.

The buyer will most likely visit in person one or more times to inspect your facilities and business processes. They may want to meet key team members. *You have the right to say no.* But if you agree, be careful to allow this only with employees who are in your innermost circle. The buyer will usually, with your permission and guidance, contact your most important clients and partners. Likely, they will talk with people who know about you, without asking your permission. All of this takes place with everyone bound by NDAs, so you can be confident that the deal's terms and business details will not leak out. But some clever clients or associates might intuit that you are engaged in a discussion to sell.

To minimize potentially damaging leaks, you can concoct

a cover story for the customer outreach questions: "We're considering a partnership or joint business venture," or, "We are surveying our best clients to rework our marketing and positioning." With respect to your important employees and touring the buyers through your facility, be very careful to set the terms for these engagements. The disruption of your day-to-day business can decrease the size of your deal, the possibility of change can cause distrust or worry in your staff, and a visit poses the risk of leaks.

Be strong in the face of your buyer's insistence to involve anyone in your company who is not already an insider to your exit plans. Have the buyer agree to specific prohibitions in the NDA, if that makes you comfortable. Above all, be very clear about the degree of secrecy you expect. You could insist that the buyers visit after business hours or on a weekend. You can ask them to use an agreed upon "cover story" when talking to others. You have a right to protect your company, employees, and customers, and a savvy buyer will respect this.

Your buyer might engage an outside accounting firm and legal support to carry out due diligence. This helps them limit the time spent by their own CFO or comptroller, and it may be necessary due to licensing requirements for attorneys (if the buyer is offshore or out of state). It may be that different legal specializations, such as employment, contract, or corporate law, are needed. In any case, the buyer is usually better equipped than you are to bear this cost. You will most likely have support from your CPA and corporate lawyer, who should be responsible enough to call in a consult if anything arises outside their expertise or jurisdiction.

Expect the due diligence phase to last up to eight weeks, excluding holidays. You can limit timeline and cost by being prepared. Use the checklist in the appendix to help you gather documents and keep them current. Feel free to ignore items that are not pertinent to your business. Talk to your CPA and attorney about their experience and their fees for supporting your interests in the transaction. They may make you a deal more favorable than their customary hourly fees—for example, a smaller fee with a final payment contingent on the success of a deal.

Talk with your CPA and any other advisers about the market valuation you've done. Are there things they notice that could add to or detract from your value in the buyer's calculation? If you notice risks, you can act to close any gaps, but at the very least you can learn to talk about those risks with the buyer in a way that highlights your management of them.

Due diligence is not fun. You will be asked to provide the same documents more than once due to an error in their transfer or someone's inattention. You will have to prepare financial statements a half dozen different ways to appease the buyer's accountant. And you will have to work hard at the same time to keep up with your regular job of running your business. If, during the years you spent growing and increasing the value of your company, you've been attentive to tight records, consistent processes, and the right team, you will make it through due diligence with minimal disruption and a buyer with few remaining concerns.

NEGOTIATION

Following completion of due diligence is the final phase of the deal: negotiating the exact terms of the contract. Your buyer may adjust terms of the deal if anything uncovered in due diligence negatively impacts their perception of your company's value. You may find yourself in a stronger position to negotiate if you've learned any particular attributes that they find attractive about your business. Remember, though, that in negotiating price in the LOI, the buyer has already determined an amount you'll accept. Your negotiations are unlikely to move this bar, but you can look for leverage on terms, such as earnouts or the length of your continued involvement after the sale.

There are only two types of negotiations: *win–win* (collaborative) and *adversarial* (competitive). Either one may result in a good deal for you, and either may happen with a strategic buyer, who wants success like you do. You might think a negotiation with a strategic buyer would always have a win–win goal, but sometimes you run up against a buyer who supports only an "I win!" deal.

In an adversarial negotiation, one party believes the value of the deal is fixed and unchangeable. Theorists call this a "distributive negotiation," but you'll also hear terms like *zero-sum game* or *win–lose*. I like the word "adversarial." It reminds me that the party across the table sees only one winner emerging in some aspect of the deal. Maybe the buyer agrees your two companies are stronger together—not a zero sum, but greater than isolated parts—but they need to triumph on some detail, such as the sale price or timing of payments for the purchase.

Win–win negotiations are sometimes called "integrative negotiations." They often have several to many components, and either side can make trade-offs to achieve a balance. Both sides will be more willing to do so if the perceived additive value of the companies is great enough.

Do whatever you can to understand what negotiating with this buyer might be like at the LOI stage. This is not always possible, and you may be surprised later. Keep in mind that nothing is wrong with either negotiating style, and you can do well in either case. But you will achieve the best deal only when you understand which type of negotiation you're engaging in.

I usually enter negotiations looking for a win–win. That's just my preference, and it's not meant to imply that I'm nicer or fairer than others. In a perceived win–win negotiation, my job is twofold: (1) I track each negotiating point and try to understand if the buyer is moving toward an adversarial position on any of them, and (2) I try to maximize the buyer's excitement about the potential in the deal, looking for factors beyond the dollar value or the future value of the combined companies, and I seek to uncover hidden factors like prestige or personal accomplishment.

When I sold my last company, one unstated but important factor in the deal was my Canadian buyer's desire to acquire a US corporation to simplify taxation as their US revenue grew. In negotiations, you'll exercise the skills you honed as a salesperson, questioning the buyer about their problems, their goals, and the impact this acquisition will help them achieve. This is gap analysis—the buyer, just like a customer, will articulate a need ("We're looking to add to our capabilities in this technology"), but not a problem ("Revenues have been somewhat flat, so we hope an acquisition will pay back beyond our investment"). Note that the *problem* provides all kinds of opportunities for more questions, while the *need* does not.

If you sense at any time that the negotiation becomes adversarial, you will not succeed in bringing the buyer to a win–win conversation. You should immediately recognize that, for whatever reason, the buyer believes they need to win something and you have to lose something. The classic response to this—if it's discovered before negotiations have gone too far—is to up your price. Let the buyer force you lower, to accept what you would have accepted at the outset. Make it clear that accepting less is difficult or painful for you, so they view your acceptance of their price as a loss.

Unfortunately, such business deals are usually not this simple. Sellers often enter negotiations with a strategic buyer, assuming the buyer sees the advantage of a win–win, only to find they must lose something dear to them or walk away from the table. Walking away can be costly, but it can reset the conversation to a point of similar advantage—not to a win–win, but to a similar understanding. You do not want to be the smaller, less powerful party and on the back foot. This buyer courted you at the beginning, spending time and money to get this far in the deal, and you've been talking nonstop about the great things you'll achieve together. They want you. Make it so they ask you to come back to the table.

This reset is more than just a repositioning strategy. Your buyer is still an adversarial negotiator. However, now you know that, and you can work to develop some leverage to deal with their need to win. For example, you might accept a lower price but insist on better earnout terms, a higher salary in your employment contract, or their paying your deal costs. These are part of your value equation and may be easier for the buyer to swallow—perhaps their board measures success by the sales price exclusively.

Note that most negotiations are not adversarial. If you're accustomed to understanding your customer's gaps, you'll likely be successful understanding your buyer's as well. A buyer with no gaps is not a strategic buyer, and you will likely learn up front exactly what terms they will accept in the deal. This is a great situation for a seller. If the terms work for you, you can close the deal with no negotiating at all. If they don't, you can say "no thanks" with zero remorse. Working out a great deal with a strategic buyer is more complex, but when you're working to define that win–win scenario, it can be a lot of fun.

YOUR FUTURE AS THE OWNER

To hedge against the risk of acquiring a business that is not substantially independent of the owner, buyers use several tactics. These tactics are so common when acquiring smaller companies that you should expect to see them proposed even if your company is mature enough to function independently. The difference is that if you've done the work, you'll have a much easier time negotiating these to more favorable outcomes.

First, buyers will require that you contract to stay with the company, usually with a two- to five-year commitment to the new owners. The contract terms may specify later vesting of stock or a downstream bonus. The rewards are normally weighted toward the end of the contract term.

Second, some buyers will promise you anything to get you to stay on. If your goal in the sale is a smooth transition for your employees, they will promise that you retain control of hiring and firing, bonuses, and strategic direction. They may promise that you can make, at your discretion, investments in new equipment or facilities, so long as you stay on as part of the team. Unfortunately, none of these promises is binding, so be aware that things may be different once the new owners have control.

At worst, promises will be broken, even before you leave, by new owners willing to push or test your loyalty. The new owners will suddenly find you're not as profitable as they expected, possibly because they disrupted your smoothly running company by setting new tasks and objectives for you. They'll point out that all their promises of your having full control were predicated on your increasing profitability. Your hopes to grow faster face new hurdles with the new owners, and your employees may wonder what happened. Some terms you promised your team in the transition may prove impossible for you to deliver.

Trying to run your business to meet the expectations of a new set of owners can be very challenging.

Buyers often use a milestone payment called an *earnout* as an incentive for you to stay. Let's say you sell your company for $5 million. The buyer offers you $2.5 million at closing, $1 million after one year if you hit a profit target, another million for a profit target at the end of year two, and $1.5 million if you hit a target in year three—a total of $6 million instead of the original $5 million if you stay on and meet some goals. The buyer proposes it as a risk-sharing arrangement, and what rewards you'll get! Who better to hit these targets than you, the one who built this great company from scratch? The targets are often based on the glowing predictions *you* made when you sold. "Look at the great potential here!" you said.

Earnouts are tricky. The buyer will gain control of your books, and by moving money around (for example, combining back-office expenses with other subsidiaries and putting the total on *your* income statement), they can effectively prevent you from hitting the agreed-upon profit targets. The buyer might keep you busy with the integration of their companies, in training their other subsidiaries to sell what you do, or in administrative meetings. With all the extra responsibility, your efficiency decreases and you miss targets. Some surveys indicate that more than 60 percent of owners who agree to earnouts as part of their acquisition do not receive the hoped-for compensation.

CLOSING THE DEAL

Much like closing on the sale of a house, closing on a business sale involves many signatures on many documents. Unlike with a house, though, your business deal usually involves a continuing relationship between you and your buyer. Others are involved, too—your employees, family, customers, vendors, and others will be affected to varying degrees. Most founders feel personally invested in the companies they build. Although as a successful seller you'll be proud of what you achieved, you will probably see it as your responsibility to shape the coming transition, to the degree you can, to the benefit of your employees who helped you get there.

> Being able to exit feels like a success. I had seventeen years into this, and we were growing. But there had been some tough periods, and I knew that eventually this was going to affect my health and life.
>
> Four years before we were acquired, we had accepted this was the course, and we started to plan for it. The planning was more active during the last year or two. We had one offer that didn't pan out—we ultimately decided it wasn't the right fit—and that process taught us a lot. When the right buyer came along, we were ready.
>
> You have to get to that point psychologically, and then you have to plan for it. There are probably some gaps that you need to fill to get a good deal, things you need to do to get there.
>
> We had a really good attorney and an accountant that helped a lot. Having long relationships with them, where they knew us well, was valuable. They didn't make a lot of money off us for a long time, but they got a good return in the end!
>
> Dr. Robert Suto
>
> Founder and CEO, Xtal BioStructures

Plan a way to tell your employees and to introduce them to the new owners. Don't just wing this—make the announcement celebratory. Remember that your employees' performance and loyalty are components of what brought you to this deal. Your employees represent a good part of the value of your business, for which your buyer just paid a handy sum. Thank these staffers and reward them.

If, so far, you are engaged in a good working relationship with the new owners, you may have already developed an integration plan. If not, this will be your first action. Think in terms of the *first one hundred days*, a time frame that seems to capture people's imagination when they think of a leadership transition. This is the time frame and phrase the media often use in describing the early actions of a new president of the United States. Certain tasks will have priority, such as changing signatories on bank accounts. Some things will be initiated, such as changing to a new accounting system or CRM application. Customers will have to be informed of any changes to the business procedures. You can probably hold off for a little while on things like changing the corporate brand, website, or employee email addresses. But whatever is to be done, someone must be accountable for each task and timelines should be set.

Transition planning is not simple. For example, imagine your bookkeepers are no longer necessary staff, as your buyer has an internal accounting group and a comptroller. Great, that will save money—it's part of the reason this deal is good for both sides. But this is not a trivial transition, and like all changes it requires some thought. Give your bookkeepers and accountant notice. Make sure your administrative personnel know how to get bills paid and are trained on new accounting procedures and software. Transfer all historical data. Establish communications processes. Make sure you're still getting monthly close reports so you can execute properly. Learn how to make a capital purchase and follow the new approval process. Establish new purchasing procedures for your team. Get budgets for the current year and the template for next year. And so on.

Every process not exclusive to your business can be adapted to harmonize with the buyer's culture and process. It just takes thought and work. If you can establish measurables to determine if a transition task is complete, you can assign it to a team member. Drive toward completion. Often in transitions, tasks remain incomplete, so a smoothly operating process remains out of reach. This creates stresses that may be invisible at first but always show up later in the form of unhappy employees and poorly functioning cross-organizational relationships.

You, and others who worked to get the deal done, will feel worn out and deserving of a vacation when the deal closes. Take your much deserved break, but come back prepared to take on the hard work needed to integrate two organizations to achieve the goal of making a sum greater than its parts.

KEY TAKEAWAYS FROM CHAPTER 15

- While you can shut down your business or transfer it to family, closing a deal with a buyer, whether an outsider or an insider, is more complex. Plan ahead—you may receive offers before you've even thought about selling. Consider the type of buyer you might want and the support you'll need, and prepare as much as possible for the process. If you prepare, you'll save time, get a better deal, endure less stress and hassle, and stand a better chance of transferring your company to the right new owner.
- Preparation means getting your business systems and documents in order and organized, closing up all lingering issues (lawsuits, employment claims, liens, and the like), and systematizing everything you can. Better organized owners get better deals.
- From LOI to final contract signing, you'll be negotiating terms. Use gap analysis (see Chapter 11) to understand your buyer. What problems do you solve for them, as opposed to the need they express? Is your buyer working with you

toward a win–win, or are they competing to win at the expense of your losing? How might you structure the deal in your favor, whatever the negotiation style?

CHAPTER 16

THE FINAL CHAPTER?

So, you sold the company. *Whew!*

You may have a short-term employment contract or be required to stay several years to get a full payout, depending on your desires and the buyer's and on your negotiated terms. Fewer than 10 percent of selling owners stay past the negotiated time period.

You may find it difficult after being the sole person in charge for years to now suddenly report to someone who doesn't know your company or have the same level of personal investment. The new owners may have goals and plans you didn't anticipate and don't agree with. Changes in the buyer's organizations may result in a new boss you don't like. Any of a number of realities can get in the way of a long, happy relationship with a buyer, and it's worth understanding that from the outset. Besides, you sold your company because, in some way, you wanted to make a transition. Go ahead, make it.

Knowing the end of your contract is arriving, you will probably find yourself becoming less engaged as you anticipate the end. Encourage your team and enfranchise them, help the new owners identify potential leaders, and assist in the cultural integration wherever possible. You want your legacy to be a successful exit by which the company you built continues to flourish—and the employees you hired and invested in continue to be happy.

If your buyer—your new boss—indicates they would like you to stay but you don't intend to, I recommend giving notice at least three and possibly six months in advance of the end of a multiyear contract. This, of course, presumes your contract protects you from losing salary, bonuses, or a final payment from the sale of your company—and your attorney, with whom you discussed your plans, should have helped you ensure this.

Assuming there's no reason to be protective about the news that you're leaving, it benefits everyone to know this final part of the transition is going to happen. Your team and the new owners will be able to best work with you to protect their roles and investments. If, on the other hand, you are not protected by a contract and might face a loss of an important payment or income if you give six months' notice, beware of revealing your intentions. If you don't have such a contract, you don't owe the owners anything. By failing to set up a mutually beneficial arrangement, they did a bad job of ensuring your cooperation.

I could never be an employee again. Even if there were a corporate job that would earn me a lot more money, I would never be able to take it. The control and immediacy elements are too important to me. I could never go back to being an employee.

But I sort of hate that I can never walk away. There have been some really tough, dark times in running this company, and I would tell myself that I can always quit and go get a job...but in the end I can't do that. That's what's hard about this life. There's no escape, and it's mostly from inside me—I could never stop. I know I'm not alone. Everyone I talk to has the same challenges and feels the same anxiety, and it helps to know that. I've accepted it, and accepting it means knowing I love it.

I suspect that if I exit, I'll do it again. The problem is that the ideas never stop, and that's too hard to stay away from. I tell myself I'll stop and enjoy life, but it's too strong.

Laura Browne

CEO, Covalent Bonds

WHAT NOW?

In many ways, after the sale of your business, you're starting something new just as you did when you founded your company. You may be on your way out, to a new home in the mountains or on the shore. Or maybe you'll take an extended vacation before starting a new company—it is likely easier the second time around! Either way, you built something of beauty and value that is worthy of your pride, and in selling it you validated your efforts. Just like a child leaving college to launch a career, your hard work paid off. Moreover, you left a mark on the world.

Don't underestimate the significance of your accomplishment. You have probably been focused for some time on closing this deal and making sure your operation is healthy postacquisition. You've consulted advisers and maybe other owners who've made similar transitions. You might assume that lots of owners have been down this road before you, but in reality, only a few make it. The cycle of starting, growing, and selling a company is achieved only by a handful of business owners, so you are part of an elite group. Through courage and perseverance—what business gurus call *grit*—you learned and did what you needed to become much more than just an expert in your field. You became an entrepreneur and built a company that has value beyond your expertise—a thriving business that became the envy of others and the strategic goal of a rich buyer.

You probably had some luck, you made some good choices and bad, you recovered from mistakes, and you found good people and inspired them to believe in your vision. You asked dumb questions and received good advice along the way. All of these require grit, so if you doubted yourself along the way, you can stop doubting now.

It's time to raise a glass of your favorite sparkling beverage, toast to everyone present, and remember all those who believed in you and still do. You are a success, and you deserve this moment.

ACKNOWLEDGMENTS

I wrote this book out of love for those who, like me, risked or will risk everything on the belief that they know or have something that others value. For experts like us, creating a business from our expertise is so tantalizing and yet at times completely unimaginable. I knew everything (well, a good bit anyway) about chemistry's uses in drug development. I knew next to nothing about starting and running a business. Thankfully, I realized that only in hindsight!

I thank the many people who tolerated my naive questions over the years as I learned: Kerry Spear, Tom Wagler, Scott Leonard, Jim Vath, Bud Weller, and others who were early customers even though they knew my team and I were still figuring out how to operate efficiently. Joe Barendt, Ronan Cleary, and Todd Palcic—and others—who, as equipment vendors and suppliers, believed we would ultimately succeed and become a showcase for their products. Rod Cole, who—without irony—celebrated the first lab I opened, even when all I could show him in that lab was a squirt bottle full of alcohol for cleaning glassware. Judy Carmody, Steve Guyan, Janet Wolfe, Jim Jersey, and all the other founders of similar companies in the Boston area—I bugged them endlessly for stories, connections, and tips. Their generosity was bottomless, and I try to follow their example every day.

I owe a special thank-you to Peter Glick, a founder and an investor, who met with me on a very dark morning in 2009, soon after the Great Recession began. I was almost out of cash and desperate for a savior. I nearly begged Peter to help me find one, or to float me himself. He looked at my accounts and financial statements and said, "You've got enough for two pay periods. Why don't you just go try to make a couple of big sales?" That was exactly what I needed to hear to pull up my suspenders and succeed. I landed a big deal, got half the fee up front, and never looked back.

Thanks also to Walt Wright, my corporate attorney and longtime adviser, from whom I learned much about the M&A process. Walt and I shared frustrations and fun as we crafted a workable deal when I sold my last company in 2016. And he is always good for a story about the Boston Red Sox in the old days.

Finally, the greatest thanks to my wife, Katy, without whom I would never have had enough faith in myself—and courage—to undertake my entrepreneurial journey. I hope you, the reader of this book, have someone to believe in you as much as Katy believes in me.

I wish you every lucky break, every generous colleague and mentor, every loyal customer, and every bit of grit I had.

APPENDIX

DUE DILIGENCE CHECKLIST

Below is a comprehensive list of items and information that may be requested in the due diligence phase of a corporate acquisition. Expect a potential buyer to ask for everything and more, and allow yourself to be pleasantly surprised if their list is not this long!

It might seem odd to finish with a checklist developed by some investment banker or MBA—it's not really in line with the practical and conversational tone of the rest of the book. If you use this to guide your thinking during discussions with a buyer, great. But my reason for including it is a little less direct. If you've followed along on this journey from startup and growth to see a maturing company emerge—one that you worked on instead of in—this checklist can help you identify gaps you want to fill or things you want to fix. It will also help you see just how much you've achieved. I recommend you use it as a self-evaluation tool: a tool that helps you see all that you've built, and a guide to bring you through any last things you want to have in place as you embark on your next steps—whatever they are!

KEY DUE DILIGENCE ACTIVITIES

CATEGORY AND CHECKLIST	APPLICABLE?	NOTES
FINANCIAL MATTERS		
Three years' annual statements, quarterly (ideally monthly) for past period		
Are statements audited?		
Are current and contingent liabilities listed?		
Margin growth		
Projections for current year		
Is the budget board approved?		
Working capital requirement		
Seasonality of working capital requirement		
Working capital agreement for acquisition		
Anticipated Capex current and next year		
Condition of assets		
Liens on assets		
Outstanding long-term liabilities to company		
Unusual revenue recognition conditions (describe)		
Any deferred capital expenditures?		
Capital and operating budgets appropriate		
Calculation of EBITDA appropriate		
Can company continue ordinary operations during period prior to close date?		

CATEGORY AND CHECKLIST	APPLICABLE?	NOTES

TECHNOLOGY/IP

Domestic and foreign patents		
Material exceptions or other IP protection concerns		
Appropriate NDAs and legal protections		
Appropriate assignment agreements with employees/partners		
Registered or common-law trademarks or service marks		
Dependence on maintenance of trade secrets		
Potential infringement on third-party IP		
IP litigation or disputes		
Technology in-licenses		
Licenses granted to third parties		
Open-source software use or issues		
List any licensed software (other than office software) that is critical to operations		
Indemnities to/from third parties with respect to IP disputes		
Liens or encumbrances on company IP		

CUSTOMERS/SALES

List top twenty customers and revenues generated from each		
Customer concentration issues		
Issues in retaining customers		
Customer satisfaction with company		

CATEGORY AND CHECKLIST	APPLICABLE?	NOTES
Warranty issues with current or past customers		
Customer backlog		
Sales terms, levels of returns or refunds		
Sales staff compensation		
Effect of acquisition on sales team financial incentives		
Seasonality of revenue		

STRATEGIC FIT WITH BUYER

	APPLICABLE?	NOTES
Estimated fit (high/medium/low)		
Does company have products/ services/tech buyer does not have?		
Can key people be retained after closing?		
Estimated timeline for integration		
Estimated cost of integration		
Savings/synergies expected in integration		
Marginal costs (e.g., obtaining third-party consents) generated by acquisition		
Estimated revenue enhancements postacquisition		

MATERIAL CONTRACTS

	APPLICABLE?	NOTES
Guaranties, loans, credit agreements		
Customer or supplier contracts		
Partnerships or joint ventures		
Operating agreements, LLCs, etc.		
Contracts with outstanding payments		

CATEGORY AND CHECKLIST	APPLICABLE?	NOTES
Settlement agreements		
Past acquisition agreements		
Indemnification agreements		
Equipment leases		
Employment agreements		
Exclusivity agreements		
Restrictions on company's rights to compete in a business or a region		
Real estate leases or purchase agreements		
License agreements		
Powers of attorney		
Franchise agreements		
Equity finance agreements		
Union contracts or collective bargaining agreements		
Any contract that, on termination, would result in a material adverse impact on company		
Approvals required of other parties in the event of a change of control		
EMPLOYEE/ MANAGEMENT ISSUES		
Original chart, key employee bios		
Summary of any current or previous labor disputes		
Employment and consulting agreements		
Docs describing transactions with officers, directors, key employees, etc.		

CATEGORY AND CHECKLIST	APPLICABLE?	NOTES
Officer, director, and key employees summary of cash and noncash compensation past two years		
Summary employee benefits, pension, profit sharing, deferred compensation, retirement plans		
Stock options or similar plans—compliance with IRS sec 409A		
Other management incentive or bonus plans, cash or noncash		
Need for compliance with IRS sec 280G (golden parachute) rules?		
Employee handbook, policies, manuals		
Involvement of any employee or officer in criminal or significant civil litigation		
Severance, termination pay, vacation, sick leave, extensions of credit, relocation assistance, educational assistance, benefits, workman's comp, executive compensation, or fringe benefits—summarize		
Are personnel appropriately treated as contractors/ employees per IRS rules?		
Employee retention agreements		
Layoffs and severance costs (estimated) associated with acquisition		
LITIGATION		
Filed or pending litigation, including complaints or pleadings		
Litigation settled and terms of settlement		

CATEGORY AND CHECKLIST	APPLICABLE?	NOTES
Claims threatened against company		
Consent decrees, injunctions, judgments against company		
Attorneys' letters to company or auditors		
Insurance covering any claims, notices to insurance carriers		
Matters in arbitration		
Pending or threatened governmental proceedings against company		
TAX MATTERS		
Federal, state, local, foreign income returns (including sales tax) filed in past five years		
Government audits		
Net operating loss or credit carryforwards		
IRS form 5500 for 401(k) plans		
Agreements, including settlements or waivers, pertinent to tax liabilities		
Has buyer consulted with own accountant with respect to tax issues in purchase?		
ANTITRUST OR REGULATORY ISSUES		
Scope of any antitrust issues		
Does the acquisition require approval of a regulator?		
Has company been involved in any prior antitrust or regulatory investigations?		
Are Hart-Scott-Rodino thresholds applicable?		

CATEGORY AND CHECKLIST	APPLICABLE?	NOTES
Does the transaction involve foreign investment issues that may apply Exon-Florio?		
Department of Commerce filings required if buyer is a foreign entity		
INSURANCE		
Extent of self-insurance arrangements		
General liability		
D&O insurance		
IP insurance		
Auto insurance		
Health insurance		
E&O insurance		
Key man insurance		
Employee liability insurance		
Worker's comp insurance		
Umbrella policies		
GENERAL CORPORATE MATTERS		
Charter documents		
Tax authority certificate of good standing		
Charter documents of any subsidiaries		
List of jurisdictions in which company and subsidiaries are qualified to do business		
Current officers and directors list		
List of all security holders (common, preferred, options, warrants)		

CATEGORY AND CHECKLIST	APPLICABLE?	NOTES
Stock option agreements and plans		
Warrant agreements		
Stock sale agreements		
Stock appreciation rights or related grants		
Grants of restricted stock units		
Stockholder and voting agreements		
Records of all other stock-related rights		
Dividend or dividend restriction agreements		
If securities were issued, evidence of compliance with securities laws and filing documents		
Recapitalization or restructuring documents		
Agreements to any sales or purchases of businesses		
"Nonshop" or exclusivity obligations		
Rights of first refusal in connection with sale of company or subsidiary businesses		
Minutes of stockholder meetings including written consents to actions without a meeting		
Minutes of board of director's meetings		

ENVIRONMENTAL ISSUES

Audits, records, reports for each owned or leased property		
Tests or audits of neighboring facilities if required by regulatory authority		

CATEGORY AND CHECKLIST	APPLICABLE?	NOTES
Hazardous substance inventory		
Permits and licenses		
Notices, correspondence, files related to EPA, state, or local authorities		
Litigation, claims, or investigations		
Superfund exposure		
Contingent environmental liabilities or indemnification obligations		
Petroleum products on site, other than in passenger vehicles		
Asbestos contained in any improvements located on the company's properties		
Records from any public agency's investigation of the company's or neighboring properties with respect to environmental regulations		
RELATED PARTY TRANSACTIONS		
Any interest of any officer, director, or stockholder in a competitive or customer business of the company		
Any compensation agreements with any officer, director, or stockholder		
Any agreements in which an officer, director, or stockholder has an interest in any company asset or property		
REGULATIONS, FILINGS, COMPLIANCE		
Citations or notices received, since inception or with continuing effect		
Pending or threatened investigations		

CATEGORY AND CHECKLIST	APPLICABLE?	NOTES
Material correspondence with any agency or entity such as FDA, USDA, EPA, or OSHA		
Documents showing compliance or deficiency with respect to any regulatory standards applying to the company		
Reports on burdens and costs of compliance (ERISA, labor, other state/local/federal)		
Material permits and licenses required to carry out business of the company or subsidiaries		
Information on cancellation or revocation of any license or permit		
Evidence of exemption from any permit or license requirement		

PROPERTY

Deeds, leases, deeds of trust, mortgages		
Title reports		
Other interests in real property		
Financing leases and sale and leaseback agreements		
Conditional sale agreements		
Operating leases		

PRODUCTION RELATED MATTERS

List of significant subcontractors and dollar value of business with each		
List of largest suppliers, and amount purchased during most recent fiscal year and YTD		

CATEGORY AND CHECKLIST	APPLICABLE?	NOTES
Monthly manufacturing yield summary by product		
Schedule of backlog by customer and product		
Inventory reports		
Any materials or supply subject to shortages		
Contracts with key subcontractors or service providers		
Agreements related to R&D, manufacturing, and testing of company's products		

MARKETING ARRANGEMENTS

Sales rep, distributor, agent, or franchise agreements		
Standard company sales forms and literature, including price lists, catalogs, POs, etc.		
Surveys or markets the company serves or plans to serve if available		
Press releases concerning the company or its business relationships		

COMPETITIVE LANDSCAPE

Principle current competitors		
Technology threats		
Competitive advantage of the company's products and technologies versus competitors		

ONLINE DATA ROOM

Seller agrees to process and to timeline for due diligence		

CATEGORY AND CHECKLIST	APPLICABLE?	NOTES
Data room TOC or directory is easily understood and has text search capabilities		
Buyer is allowed to print documents for offline review and share with collaborators under NDA		
Ideally a disclosure schedule is provided by the buyer and complied with		
Updates to the data room are clearly marked and trigger email notification to buyer and counsel		

www.ingramcontent.com/pod-product-compliance
Lightning Source LLC
Chambersburg PA
CBHW030454210326
41597CB00013B/667